MW01236312

Leading
the Jesus Way

Learning to Lead from the Master

Matt McCraw

To Thom—Thank you for believing in me.

For the church, to the glory of God alone.

Acknowledgements

This book would not be possible without the support of my bride, Jennifer. She's my biggest supporter, most faithful friend, and most honest critic. Jenny—I would not want to write this book without you by my side. I love you.

I'm grateful for my sons and their patience as Dad tried to find a few extra minutes here and there to do a little writing, editing, and more editing. Jeremiah, Levi, and Samuel—I'm so blessed that God gave me each of you. Try to be like Jesus in the way that you lead and in all that you do.

I'm proud to be the pastor of First Baptist Church of Bartow, Florida. They accepted me as a young man with no senior pastor experience. They let me learn along the way and spread my leadership wings the widest they'd ever been spread. I'm honored to pastor God's people in Bartow.

I'm so thankful for the leaders who have influenced me along the way. Some are named in this book, but there are so many more. To every person who took time to invest in me—thank you. Thank you for your patience. Thank you for your persistence. Thank you for your wisdom. Thank you for your grace.

To the Church Answers team—What a joy it is to work with you. You are brilliant, you are nimble, and you have a Jesus-like passion for local churches. Thanks for allowing me to work with you. Thank you particularly to Chuck Lawless for your careful consideration of this book. Your wisdom, experience, and patience have greatly improved this work. To Thom and Sam Rainer—Wow, thank you. Thank you for everything.

Contents

Introduction

I REMEMBER MY FIRST CHURCH OFFICE. I was twenty-three years old, serving as a youth pastor in southwest Florida. As a ministry intern in seminary, I shared an office with a lot of other guys, but this office was all mine. Really, it was little more than a workroom or closet. The church was actually in the middle of a remodel of their building, so this was temporary. But it was mine.

I was so excited to be in full-time ministry. I had trained and studied for five and a half years, and now I was out there in the world of ministry. I was eager to *lead*. I believed that God could use me to lead his people, and I couldn't wait to get started.

There was one major issue, though: I didn't have much experience at actually leading people. Sure, I had some experience. I learned some methodology in seminary. I gained some experience as an intern. I even led a small group of employees in my first job, but I had never led on this level.

That was seventeen years ago. As the years have gone on, I have learned how immensely challenging leadership is. I had to learn how to show compassion to staff members while also calling them to greater excellence. I had to learn how to recruit new small group leaders after half of the church left before I became pastor. I had to learn how to navigate my church through the global pandemic of 2020 and beyond. Leadership is difficult.

There are so many leadership "experts" who espouse different ideas and methodologies that the leadership waters have become cloudy. In addition, some famous church leaders, many I considered effective leaders, have fallen from leadership or no longer even claim to be followers of Jesus.

To add to the problem, leaders in our culture often lead with threatening control, dominating arrogance, or immoral and conniving methods.

Local churches are in real need of leaders who lead the Jesus way.

Churches are closing every day. Conversion numbers are down in many Christian denominations. Some "leaders" lead out of hubris and lust for power. There is an urgent need for leaders to commit to lead the Jesus way. I want to be the kind of leader Jesus uses to lead his people.

I don't want to be a clueless leader. I don't want to be an ineffective and unproductive leader. I want to be a leader who gets stuff done, but I want to get that stuff done the right way. I don't want to be immoral. I don't want to be arrogant. I want to be like Jesus. I want to lead the Jesus way.

We can be like Jesus in many ways, including leading like Jesus. That is good news for you and me. One of the amazing miracles of the gospel is that by the power of the Holy Spirit we can become more and more like our savior, Jesus Christ. The apostle Paul tells us in 2 Corinthians 5:15, "This means that anyone who belongs to Christ has become a new person. The old life is gone; a new life has begun!" In Jesus, we have new life. The old way of things has passed. We can be more like Jesus in the way we love, in the way we live, and in the way we lead. That is what this book is all about: leading the Jesus way. Let's begin a journey to discover how you can lead like the greatest leader of all time!

Seeing True Leadership in Jesus

The encouraging reality is that followers of Jesus have a unique source of wisdom for leadership effectiveness. All we have to do is look at Scripture, which shines a spotlight on the greatest leader of all time: Jesus Christ of Nazareth. This book will take you to Jesus for timeless leadership lessons that will transform you to be the leader God has called you to be.

In order to lead the Jesus way, we must place a priority not only on discovering Jesus-like leadership but also on living it out. We have to make a conscious decision to be more like Jesus than the leaders of this world. We likely need to shift the way we develop our leadership strategies. Instead of trying to display more power, we need to display more humility. Instead of expecting people to serve us, we need to learn to serve others. Instead of trying to make the most popular decision, we need to lead with conviction. Instead of seeking our own will, we must seek the will of God and the good of others. This is the kind of leadership that God intends for his church, and this is the kind of leadership that brings him glory in the life of his leaders. This is the Jesus kind of leadership.

Learning about Chainsaws and Leadership

I love to learn how to do new things. When it comes to a task about which I know nothing, I prefer to learn by watching someone complete the task (preferably someone who really knows what they're doing). A particular task I really enjoyed learning was cutting wood using a chainsaw. To be clear, I am not an expert chainsaw operator. However, one of my best friends happens to be a forester in Kentucky who *is* a chainsaw expert. With his chainsaw mastery, Jim Bryan the forester can lay a tree down exactly where he wants it.

I've spent a lot of time with Jim in the woods, and I've seen him cut a lot of trees. I'm usually glad to just be the guy who slings the limbs away after Jim cuts them down. However, I've learned to use a chainsaw—at least somewhat—by watching Jim. Watch the expert and learn—that's my chainsaw game plan.

You and I can learn leadership lessons the same way. We can learn from other Christlike leaders, and more importantly, we can learn from Jesus himself. This book will examine the leadership of Jesus to see how we can better use the gifts he's given us for the work to which he's called us. *Leading the Jesus Way* will magnify the leadership of Jesus on display in the Scriptures and provide a roadmap for how we can be like Jesus in the way we lead.

The Leadership Fruit Found in God's Word

Fortunately, many leadership lessons from Jesus are readily available for us to discover in the Word of God. It's a miracle that we have the New Testament to tell us about the life of Jesus, the teachings of Jesus, and the lasting impact of Jesus upon his early followers. The apostle John tells us in John 1:14, "So the Word became human and made his home among us. He was full of unfailing love and faithfulness. And we have seen his glory, the glory of the Father's one and only Son." What a gift it is that the Son of God made his home among us. In him, we are blessed to see the greatest leader the world has ever seen.

In order to show the leadership of Jesus, this book will focus on the New Testament Gospels (Matthew, Mark, Luke, and John). These first-hand accounts of the life of Jesus, as well as reflections upon the ministry of Jesus, will provide invaluable raw data from the divine displays of Jesus. So, let us pick this low-hanging leadership fruit by studying the life and ministry of Jesus.

Jesus Has the Answers to Our Leadership Questions

Leaders are looking for answers to their leadership questions. This book will not simply take leadership principles of the world and put them through a sanctification process. Instead, this book will show you how Jesus led during his time on the earth. This book will package and present what the Bible tells us about the leadership of Jesus in a way that is easily understandable for leaders in the church today.

As we look at the leadership of Jesus, we will see that Jesus came to the earth in obedience to the Father in order to influence, develop, change, forgive, equip, and deploy people. We will see the Jesus leadership pathway by following guideposts along the way. These guideposts will show us how leading like Jesus prioritizes people, identifies and meets needs, teaches people, develops others, calls us to persevere during opposition, and makes us people of priorities.

This Book is for You

The lessons I've learned from the leadership of Jesus have changed my life and ministry—they're still changing me. I've developed clarity and confidence in my leadership. I've made the ways of Jesus my goal rather than the ways of this world. I've learned how people were changed by the leadership of Jesus and I learned that, by God's power, they can be changed through my leadership, too.

I believe this book will be helpful for you because the lessons in *Leading the Jesus Way* are from the greatest leader of all time! I also pray that this book will be pleasing to Jesus. He wants to see us develop into better leaders. He has a heart to see competent and godly leaders serve his church. As Paul told the church in Ephesus in Ephesians 4:11–13,

> Now these are the gifts Christ gave to the church: the apostles, the prophets, the evangelists, and the pastors and teachers. Their responsibility is to equip God's people to do his work and build up the church, the body of Christ. This will continue until we all come to such unity in our faith and knowledge of God's Son that we will be mature in the Lord, measuring up to the full and complete standard of Christ.

Elsewhere, Paul says that every member has a part to play in the development of the church. In 1 Corinthians 12:27 he says, "All of you together are Christ's body, and each of you is a part of it." Every church member should be serving in some way. God's design for some of those members, though, is that they serve as leaders for the benefit of everyone in the church. What a beautiful reality—and great responsibility for those of us who lead.

God wants to use you to lead his people. Now is the time for you to sharpen your leadership skills by honing them to look more like the leadership of Jesus. Now is the time for you to take a deep dive into the Word of God and discover how you can lead like the greatest leader of all time. Keep reading and learn what it looks like to lead the Jesus way.

1
Making People a Priority

MEET JASON. JASON HAS BEEN PASTOR of Granlee Community Church for two years. He loves the people of his church. He feels the need to be more pastoral to those God has entrusted to his care. Yet, Jason has a challenge.

It's a challenge common to Christian leaders in multiple roles and organizations. Jason is just too busy. He can't get his work done. Each day ends with a longer to-do list. The demands for his time are constant and range from the trivial to the urgent.

Jason will readily admit he is task driven. He is currently working with church leaders to get the church budget finalized. He helps lead a local pastors' fellowship. The church is about to move forward with some renovation plans, and he has been meeting with the building committee and several different contractors. That's just the beginning of the list. He is frustrated with the slow progress. Jason's frustration has even led to him being a bit snippy with his wife and children. He knows it is wrong to take out his frustrations on those he loves the most.

Ultimately, what is slowing down Jason most are the people demands. Requests for pastoral care seem never-ending. Lately, the men's ministry has been asking him to be more involved with the men of the church. Weddings and funerals are part of the pastor's ministry, but he had no idea there would be so many. Others in his church just want to talk and hang out. He would like to spend time with some of these people, but it seems impossible.

As Jason takes a few minutes to pray at the end of the day, he asks God to give him wisdom to manage his time and priorities. Admittedly, Jason was really asking God to show him how to get his tasks done. But as he prays, the pastor sees the faces of those who have asked for his time. He sees the people in his church and in his life.

Jason is struck with immediate conviction. Is his problem a task problem or a people problem? Ministry is messy, and it gets even messier when people are involved. But what is he supposed to do? Even more, what would Jesus do?

Jesus Prioritized People

There's a humorous saying in ministry circles that pastors often share with each other: "Ministry would be easy if it didn't involve people." Many Christian leaders can probably identify with that statement. However, we must remember this truth: ministry is about people.

Jesus was a people person. Perhaps he was not the kind of *people person* who comes to mind when you hear that phrase. Jesus was not necessarily an outgoing person who was always the life of the party. However, he did have a special connection with people. His connectedness to people had less to do with whether he was an extrovert or an introvert and more with the reality that he prioritized people. Although none of us can be fully like Jesus (after all, he is the divine Son of God), one of the ways we can be like Jesus is by truly valuing other people.

I remember the first time I met one of my mentors, Jimmy Scroggins. I was just eighteen years old. It was at a lunch after Sunday morning worship. I was hoping to become a ministry intern at the church where Jimmy was a youth pastor. When I met him, he impressed me with a magnetic presence about him that was warm and inspirational. However, more than that, I was moved by the fact that Jimmy looked me in the eye and spoke to me in a way that demonstrated he cared about me. He said that he wanted me to serve in a ministry where I was passionate. He wanted me to use my gifts, talents, and passions for God's glory. Jimmy made me a priority not for his own gain but for my good and the multiplication of God's gifts in my life. He prioritized me because he knew that God loved me and wanted to use even someone like me.

Have you ever met someone like Jimmy—someone who prioritized you and showed genuine interest in you? That's the way Jesus prioritized people. When some leaders in his day—including religious ones—used people for their selfish gain, Jesus was different. He truly valued others.

To lead like Jesus, you must prioritize people simply because they are created in God's image. You must think of the ministry position that best fits them rather than the one that you most need filled. You must pause and listen to their story rather than trying to outdo them with a story of your own. When they walk into your office while you are writing an article or sermon, you must be willing to pause and look them in the eye rather than brush them off as an interruption. You must lead the Jesus way.

Jesus Attracted People

A common saying in the leadership arena is, "You're not a leader if no one is following you." That statement is simple yet profoundly true. If the rearview mirror of your leadership highway is empty, you might want to reconsider the route you are taking. Very simply, to lead the Jesus way means, in part, that you are someone others follow.

Jesus Was Magnetic

Jesus could hardly go anywhere without large crowds looking for him. Consider Mark 3:7–8: "Jesus went out to the lake with his disciples, and a large crowd followed him. They came from all over Galilee, Judea, Jerusalem, Idumea, from east of the Jordan River, and even from as far north as Tyre and Sidon. The news about his miracles had spread far and wide, and vast numbers of people came to see him." Prior to the events in this text, Jesus had a plan to go to the Sea of Galilee to teach and minister with his disciples. Developing his disciples was an important task. These guys were recruits who still needed to learn a lot, and this event was not a time where Jesus was trying to attract a large crowd. But people kept showing up. As Jesus led his new followers, more and more people were flocking to him. These people traveled slowly and intentionally from many miles away to come experience Jesus. They were drawn to him.

Jesus's teaching was one of the main reasons so many people came to see and hear from him. When they found him, it was often in the temple in Jerusalem. Synagogues (smaller religious centers and schools) were set up all over Israel, but the temple in Jerusalem was a big deal. It was an enormous structure that was the center of religious life and instruction for the Jewish faith. Many priests, leaders, and teachers visited and taught at the temple steps. Yet Jesus was not like the others. There was something distinctly attractive about him. Folks traveled far and wide, not to hear one of the other teachers but to hear Jesus.

Luke 21:37–38 recounts Jesus's teaching at the temple: "Every day Jesus went to the Temple to teach, and each evening he returned to spend the night on the Mount of Olives. The crowds gathered at the Temple early each morning to hear him." Jesus spent much time in Jerusalem, particularly during his final days. Luke says that every day Jesus would come and go from a mountain outside the city, down into the center of town. He would teach and minister in Jerusalem, leave to rest and recuperate, and then do it all over again.

When Jesus returned to town, people were already waiting for him at the temple. That sounds exhausting. Every day, being around people again and again. Jesus didn't even have a chance to get settled when he got to the temple. People gathered early to hear him. Yet, there was Jesus ready to teach and ready to minister. Why? Because he prioritized people. The magnetic leadership of Jesus drew multitudes of people to him, and he was prepared to minister to them.

Jesus Was Compelling

Andy Stanley said, "People are hesitant to abandon the status quo until a leader comes along and offers them a compelling alternative."[1] Jesus offered something that many people desired. Though they did not always fully understand his mission, he gave them something compelling: himself. If people are to be attracted to my leadership, or your leadership, we must offer them something compelling; we must offer them something different than what the world has to offer.

Jesus is always better than what the world has to offer. I don't want to be a worldly leader; I want to be a Christlike leader. If I work hard to create an attractive image, I may attract people, but that would not be as important as Jesus-like qualities in my leadership. If I work to build a personal platform, I may amass some followers, but ultimately it doesn't matter if these people follow me; they need to follow Jesus. I may come up with some clever words that move others, but nothing will impact people like the eternal impact of the words and ways of Jesus.

Think about what Jesus had to offer. He offered himself. He offered truth, healing, clarity, and love. So, how can I lead like Jesus did? I can present Jesus. The compelling alternative that people need is Jesus. The attractive ingredient that will draw people to leaders like Jesus is Jesus himself. So, offer people something that stirs them; offer them Jesus in the way you lead.

We can lead powerfully by leading others to discover Jesus, who is himself powerful. One of our new church members recently encouraged me regarding our church's commitment to offering something different to the world. She said she was looking for a church that wasn't just doing church as usual. She wanted to be a part of a church that was doing something special. She participated in one of our community outreach events and said, "This is why I came to this church! I'm so glad God led my family here!" Our church is still learning how to be the church God has called and created us to be, but this church member recognized that, more than anything else, people need the love of Jesus. She is glad to be a part of a church striving to give people the love of Jesus.

Make it a priority to be the type of leader who attracts people, not because of worldly characteristics but because the Spirit of the living God and Christlikeness are extruding from every part of your life. In the 1990s The Coca-Cola Company came up with a saying to remind their customers that their company offered the genuine article when it came

19

to colas: "Can't beat the real thing." Well, it's the same with Jesus. You can't beat the real thing. So, give people more of Jesus. Lead them the Jesus way, and they will follow.

Jesus Engaged People

Jesus had a magnetic presence, but he didn't always wait for people to come to him. He often went to the people. Leading the Jesus way means that we must also go to the people.

Jesus Was Intentional in Ministering to Sinners

Consider how Jesus went to Zacchaeus. Luke 19:1–5 tells us the story:

> Jesus entered Jericho and made his way through the town. There was a man there named Zacchaeus. He was the chief tax collector in the region, and he had become very rich. He tried to get a look at Jesus, but he was too short to see over the crowd.
>
> So he ran ahead and climbed a sycamore-fig tree beside the road, for Jesus was going to pass that way.
>
> When Jesus came by, he looked up at Zacchaeus and called him by name. "Zacchaeus!" he said. "Quick, come down! I must be a guest in your home today."

Jesus was intentional in his movement to Zacchaeus. He could have let Zacchaeus sit in that tree and admire his greatness. Jesus could have said, "If Zacchaeus wants to talk to me, he can come down to me." Some may have been hesitant to engage Zacchaeus because he was a well-known sinner. After all, Zacchaeus was a chief tax collector in his region, and tax collectors were considered notorious cheats and scoundrels during the time of Jesus. Yet, Jesus willingly and openly spent time with Zacchaeus. The results of Jesus's engagement with Zacchaeus speak for themselves. The tax collector gave half of his wealth to the poor and paid back those he cheated four times as much. Had Jesus not engaged

Zacchaeus, though, we would have missed this example of the marvelous change Jesus offers.

Zacchaeus was not the only sinner Jesus engaged. In fact, Zacchaeus was not the sole tax collector Jesus called to change. One of Jesus's own disciples, Matthew (also known as Levi), was a tax collector. Jesus didn't see Matthew as simply a sinner; he considered Matthew a candidate for life change. Jesus went to Matthew because he valued him—just as he engaged fishermen, outcasts, and others (see Matthew 4:18–22; Luke 5:27–32; Mark 1:39–45).

Jesus impacted these public sinners so much that they wanted to invite their friends to meet Jesus also. After Jesus called Matthew the tax collector to follow him, Matthew wanted to throw a party for his friends to meet Jesus: "Later, Matthew invited Jesus and his disciples to his home as dinner guests, along with many tax collectors and other disreputable sinners" (Matthew 9:10). The religious leaders weren't happy that Jesus spent time with these people (see Matthew 9:11). Yet, Jesus prioritized the people considered *scum* by the religious elite of his day.

Take a moment and reflect upon those words. Who are the people that would be considered scum in your context? We must prioritize those in society whom others consider unworthy of value. We must love them as Jesus loves them. We must love and lead the Jesus way.

It's essential to understand a crucial aspect of the process of engaging others: we must prioritize people by giving them our time. Just like you, I have a long to-do list. Someone recently said to me, "Pastor, when you get caught up on your to-do list, give me a call." I responded that I may call them once I retire. Those in ministry have a lot to do. At the risk of stating the biggest understatement of the last two thousand years, Jesus was a busy and important person. None of us has a more important ministry than he did. Our schedules are not more important than Jesus's was. Yet, Jesus still took time to engage others.

Jesus Was Sensitive to the Needs of Others

Jesus had an uncanny ability to sense the needs of people. After all, he is the Creator of all things. Once, while Jesus was in a crowd full of people and on his way to visit a dying child, he sensed that a woman had reached out and touched him. Jesus stopped everything to engage the woman and offer her healing (see Luke 8:42–48). At a different time, as he was busy with ministry, Jesus was "interrupted" by families seeking blessings for their children. Although his disciples tried to brush the families away, Jesus welcomed and engaged them (see Matthew 19:13–15). Jesus recognized the needs of these families, and he ministered to them.

I'm not naturally open to the needs of others. I'm naturally task-oriented; I'm sensitive to tasks that I've not yet completed. However, as I grow older and serve longer in ministry, God has made me more and more of a people person. Part of my development is due to my own sanctification, and part is due to learning from repeated failure. Undoubtedly, my primary source of growth has come by learning from the Master. We must also ask the Holy Spirit to soften our hearts and open our eyes to recognize the needs of others. This ability to recognize needs came naturally for the divine Son of God. Yet, we must intentionally listen for God's leading in our lives. We must continue to learn to lead the Jesus way.

Leading the Jesus way requires prioritizing people and being available for what may seem like an interruption. These "interruptions" are people made in the image of God, some who may be radically changed by the work of Jesus. You may have to put your sermon on hold. You may have to miss that lunch with your friend. You may have to lose a few extra hours of sleep. However, it's worth it. Your people need you. Others will need you. They need you to love them and lead them the Jesus way.

Jesus Was Flexible in How He Ministered

When it came to engaging people, Jesus had more than one way of going about it. He was versatile and flexible. Let's consider a few ways Jesus engaged others.

Sometimes Jesus engaged others through confrontation, as with the religious leaders of his day (see Matthew 23:27–28). We will have to confront others also. Confrontation may be necessary in your ministry when someone is causing disunity in your church, spreading false information, or walking in sin. When confrontation occurs, we must confront in a Christlike way.

At times, Jesus engaged others through spontaneously healing. Imagine being sick or disabled for many years and someone suddenly brings you healing. Such was the case with many people Jesus engaged (see John 5:1–15). Leaders like Jesus must be ready to pray for and love those who are hurting.

Jesus also engaged others through correction (see Luke 10:13–16). He often did this to help his disciples learn to become who God designed them to be. Sometimes the best way to love a church member or a fellow leader is by lovingly correcting them. Loving correction, like Jesus modeled, is rooted in genuine care.

Jesus also engaged others by calling them to repentance (see John 5:14–15). Likewise, God may use you to call someone away from a life of sin and to a life of following after him. This type of engagement characterized the life of Jesus and should undoubtedly characterize the life of someone who leads the Jesus way.

Flexibility, sensitivity, and intentionality characterized the way Jesus engaged others. So also, it must characterize how we interact with people. In every case where Jesus engaged others, it was a personal encounter. That's at the heart of leading the Jesus way: encountering and engaging people personally. You and I can lead with flexibility, as Jesus did, by always being ready to engage others and minister in his name.

If this idea of making people a priority seems intimidating, be encouraged; God will not call you to do anything he will not equip you to do. The Father has called you, Jesus has commissioned you, and the Holy Spirit will empower you to lead like Jesus. You can do it; you can lead the Jesus way by engaging others.

Jesus Shared Meals with People

I love to eat. When I was new in ministry, I never realized how biblical it is to share a meal with someone. What a joy I was missing! I now realize that I can be more like Jesus by sitting down with someone over a meal.

One of my mentors in ministry, Kevin Ezell, says, "There's no problem that Cracker Barrel can't fix." Indeed, a lot of leadership can happen over a plate of food. This idea is not new. Over two thousand years ago, Jesus led people by bringing the worlds of ministry and food together.

Jesus shared meals with different people, in different contexts, for different purposes. The common thread was food and influence. Pastor Andrew Hébert studied how Jesus used meals to influence others, and his findings are striking (see table 1.1).[2] Sharing meals with others was integral to the ministry of Jesus.

Table 1.1 Meal Scenes in Luke

Text	Meal	Cultural Components Shared
Luke 5:29–39	Eating with Levi	Beliefs, values, and behavior toward tax collectors and sinners
Luke 6:1–5	Eating with Disciples in a Field	Beliefs, values, and behavior regarding Sabbath laws
Luke 7:36–50	Eating with Simon and Teaching Forgiveness	Beliefs and behavior regarding the place of the sinful woman at the table
Luke 9:10–17	The Feeding of the 5,000	Beliefs about Jesus' identity and subsequent obedient behavior
Luke 10:38–42	The Hospitality of Mary and Martha	Values regarding the importance of listening to Jesus' words
Luke 11:37–54	Eating with a Pharisee and Denouncing Hypocrisy	Behavior regarding hypocrisy
Luke 14:1–24	Eating with a Pharisee on the Sabbath	Beliefs and behavior regarding status and humility.
Luke 15:1–32	Eating with Tax Collectors and Sinners	Behavior toward tax collectors and sinners
Luke 19:1–10	Eating with Zacchaeus	Values and behavior regarding the lost
Luke 22:14–34	The Last Supper	Values and behavior regarding humility and service
Luke 24:13–43	Eating with Disciples After the Resurrection	Beliefs about Jesus' identity

There's something about sharing a meal that communicates others are important to you. When I was a young seminary student, one of my mentors, Nat Millican, met me and another student for discipleship and development. He took time out of his busy schedule each week to meet for coffee and bagels with two young men who had quite a lot of maturing to do. We shared quality time, and I soaked up all Nat had to say. Nat had a family of his own, an important job, and other leadership responsibilities, but he made time to meet with me. I felt like a priority to him, and it changed me forever. I'm so grateful for those mornings spent with Nat, and I'm grateful that he led the Jesus way.

Shared meals really do matter. If I interact with you on social media, you will simply know that I realize you exist and have something to say to you. If I send you a text message or call you on the phone, you will probably discover that you are more than a stranger to me. However, if I invite you to a meal, you know that I have prioritized you by setting time out of my schedule to spend with you. Eating a meal with you shows I value you enough to have you to my home or join you at a restaurant.

Sharing a meal with someone also provides many unique leadership opportunities. It creates a more relaxed atmosphere, allows greater transparency, and develops opportunities for greater intimacy, all of which are crucial components in the laboratory of leadership. To be sure, eating with someone takes time and resources. However, that reminds us that leading the Jesus way takes effort. Therefore, we must make it a priority. Jesus took advantage of opportunities at meals to influence others, and so should we.

So, let this book be the motivation (and perhaps excuse) you need to plan a meal with someone you are influencing. Maybe you need to look at your calendar right now to plan a lunch appointment with someone. Grab a cup of coffee, bite into a sandwich, or fire up the grill in the name of Jesus.

Jesus Ministered to Those Others Considered Undesirable

All of us have favorites we want to spend time with. My wife, Jennifer, is my favorite. I love spending time with her. A close second is the rest of my family. My kids are a handful, but they are *my* handful. I also enjoy hanging out with extended family, a few pastor friends, and a few friends with whom I hunt and fish. These are the people I most naturally enjoy. I desire to be with them.

If you pay attention to the people that Jesus spent time with, you'll notice that he prioritized people who were not usually a priority to others. We've already seen how Jesus engaged sinners, but he also engaged other "undesirables," including women and children. These were not undesirable to Jesus. He didn't aim to hang out with the powerful, influential, and popular. Instead, Jesus spent time with the "wrong" people, the "undesirables" of his day.

These people were special to Jesus, but not because they had done something spectacular or were people of high society. They were special to Jesus simply because they were people created in God's image (see Genesis 1:27). You and I must remember that every person has value before God for the same reason. Every person is important and worthy of being a priority in your life.

One of the things I discovered when I began pastoring at my current church is that many people who are in need find their way to the doors of downtown churches, particularly when the church is just a few blocks from the county courthouse and the county jail. The fact is, I encounter so many people asking for money and other forms of assistance that I started to become numb and cold toward their needs. My temptation is often to walk the other way when these people try to ask for help.

I've learned that this is not the Jesus way. Jesus prioritized those who were not a priority to others. When I encounter people, I must remind myself that they are a priority to Jesus. When I prioritize the "undesirables," I am leading the Jesus way.

Jesus and Children

The world in which Jesus lived and ministered didn't regard children highly. In fact, many people viewed children as little more than property.

The Roman Empire (and ancient Jewish society) even allowed parents to sell their children into slavery. Society would often cast off these little ones as unimportant. Yet, these little ones were of the utmost importance to their Creator and Lord. Jesus not only taught how valuable children were, but he also backed it up with how he interacted with these little ones.

Even when children interrupted Jesus, he responded in a way that the children (and their parents) saw how important they were to Jesus. Matthew 19:13–15 illustrates how Jesus prioritized children:

> One day some parents brought their children to Jesus so he could lay his hands on them and pray for them. But the disciples scolded the parents for bothering him. But Jesus said, "Let the children come to me. Don't stop them! For the Kingdom of Heaven belongs to those who are like these children." And he placed his hands on their heads and blessed them before he left.

There is little doubt that moment stood out to those who witnessed it. Those who saw Jesus interact with these children learned from firsthand experience that children were a priority to him.

Jesus and Women

As with children, women in the ancient world were not held in much esteem. However, they were a priority to Jesus. Women did most of the household work, had very little influence, and were often treated harshly. Yet, Jesus highly valued them.

Take the story of Jesus and the Samaritan woman at the well. Jesus was at a famous well in Israel, and he was thirsty. A woman was there drawing water, and Jesus spoke to her. But, of course, Jesus was not there by accident. John records this moment in John 4:7–9:

> Soon a Samaritan woman came to draw water, and Jesus said to her, "Please give me a drink." He was alone at the time because his

disciples had gone into the village to buy some food. The woman was surprised, for Jews refuse to have anything to do with Samaritans. She said to Jesus, "You are a Jew, and I am a Samaritan woman. Why are you asking me for a drink?"

Not only did others consider it inappropriate in the first century that Jesus talked to a woman, but she was also a *Samaritan* woman. The Jews and the Samaritans didn't exactly get along, to say the least. John goes on to say that Jesus took the time to speak to this woman and went further by sharing with her the beautiful truth that he was the Messiah. This woman had access to life-changing truth because Jesus prioritized her.

Some of Jesus's closest followers were women. For example, Luke 10:38–42 describes Jesus's visit to the home of two sisters named Mary and Martha. Some of the women who followed Jesus stayed faithful to him during his arrest and crucifixion, and they were some of the first to discover that he had risen from the dead. These women were faithful to Jesus, in part, because they knew that they were a priority to him.

Still today, society looks down upon certain people marginalized by others. If we're going to lead the Jesus way, though, we need to prioritize all people, including those others might ignore. Leading like Jesus means that we see people for who they are: image bearers of God. The choice is yours. Will you be content to love only those who love you? Choose not to flow with the stream of the world's disregard for certain people. Choose to lead the Jesus way.

Conclusion

Jason, our pastor at the beginning of this chapter, decided to make some changes. First, he asked God to give him a greater love for people. He knew leading people like Jesus meant he had to spend time with people, love people, and, ultimately, prioritize people.

He also knew that God was the one who gave him his task-driven personality. But he could make it one of his tasks to learn to prioritize people.

He began to reflect on his to-do list and his calendar, and he began to prioritize people, beginning with his own family. He was more intentional in his prayer time and correspondence with others. He began to ask God to do a necessary work on his heart. Then, he would take the right actions to follow in obedience.

Jesus led by prioritizing others. Will you make the same commitments to lead like Jesus did?

The first guidepost of those who lead the Jesus way is to prioritize people. We must not only prioritize people, but we must also see and meet their needs. That's the subject of chapter 2.

Key Takeaways from This Chapter

1. Jesus led in a way that attracted people.
2. Jesus led by intentionally engaging people.
3. Jesus led by sharing meals with people.
4. Jesus led by prioritizing all people.

Action Steps for Leaders

1. Purpose in your heart that people will have a priority in your life.
2. Pray a prayer of commitment right now to prioritize people.
3. Write a list of five names of people you will encourage.
4. Seek to be kind to someone who may be a challenge to you.

2
Seeing and Meeting Needs

I USED TO BE KIND OF A JERK. No, not a blatant jerk. In fact, most people probably thought that I was a nice guy. However, on the inside, I didn't have much compassion for people. I was more committed to what I had to do than I was to the people I was serving.

I've had to learn through experience to become a person of compassion. Once, I had the task of calling a list of people to let them know that our church van would not be running due to heavy winter weather. I wasn't looking forward to the task, but as a task-oriented person, I was intent on getting it done. When I called one woman, before I had a chance to tell her about the canceled van pick-up, she began to cry. Fortunately, I was wise enough to inquire why she was upset, and she told me that she had recently been diagnosed with a severe disease. I'm ashamed to admit this, but I didn't immediately have compassion for her. It took me a minute to realize that I needed to shift what was most important to me at that moment. The news about the van could wait; this woman needed to feel love and compassion from one of her pastors. I needed to lead with compassion—the way Jesus led.

If I asked someone if they would describe me as a person of compassion, I would be afraid that the answer may sting a little—even if they did indeed see me as a "nice guy." If I asked people if they see Jesus as a person of compassion, their answer would likely be an emphatic "Yes!" Part of what made Jesus the leader we know him to be was that he possessed deep compassion. As I have journeyed to discover how I could lead the Jesus way, I've sought to emulate the compassion of the most outstanding leader of all time.

31

Jesus Had Compassionate Care

Even jerks *can* be leaders. Unfortunately, you can probably think of several well-known leaders who aren't very nice. Sometimes people are duped into following these people based on bravado, power, charisma, a paycheck, or a striking smile. However, even if you are not a jerk, you can't lead the Jesus way if you lack compassion. Jesus wasn't concerned only with himself. Quite the opposite. Jesus addressed people's needs better than anyone.

Jesus *genuinely* cared for people. Luke showed us this genuine compassion in Luke 13:34, as we hear Jesus say, "O Jerusalem, Jerusalem, the city that kills the prophets and stones God's messengers! How often I have wanted to gather your children together as a hen protects her chicks beneath her wings, but you wouldn't let me." Jesus's heart of compassion led him to weep over his people, and not just this once. We see this compassion again in Luke 19:41–42: "But as he came closer to Jerusalem and saw the city ahead, he began to weep. 'How I wish today that you of all people would understand the way to peace. But now it is too late, and peace is hidden from your eyes.'"

We've already learned that Jesus frequently engaged people. However, Jesus often looked upon people with compassion before he ever engaged their needs. For example, consider how Jesus viewed the people of the towns and villages where he ministered, according to Matthew:

> Jesus traveled through all the towns and villages of that area, teaching in the synagogues and announcing the Good News about the Kingdom. And he healed every kind of disease and illness. When he saw the crowds, he had compassion on them because they were confused and helpless, like sheep without a shepherd. He said to his disciples, "The harvest is great, but the workers are few. So pray to the Lord who is in charge of the harvest; ask him to send more workers into his fields." (Matthew 9:35–38)

Jesus didn't merely see the people of the towns and villages as towns-people and villagers. He saw them as people who were confused and in need of help. So often, we ministry leaders view people through jaded lenses. Sometimes people feel like a burden to us. Leading the Jesus way means that we must understand that people are not a burden, but they are instead *burdened*. They need someone to lead them to Jesus and help them discover that Jesus came so they may have abundant life (see John 10:10).

In fact, Jesus made it clear that if people wanted to experience compassionate love and blessings, they simply needed to come to him. He said in Matthew 11:28–30, "Come to me, all of you who are weary and carry heavy burdens, and I will give you rest. Take my yoke upon you. Let me teach you, because I am humble and gentle at heart, and you will find rest for your souls. For my yoke is easy to bear, and the burden I give you is light."

I want to notice the burdens and baggage of others so I can help them turn to Jesus to find rest. I want to recognize the businessman who is spending all his time and energy on seeking the successes of the world so I can lead that man to Jesus to seek heavenly treasures and find rest for his soul (see Matthew 6:20). I want to help a struggling mother at her wits' end because she is giving all her energy to provide for her children by leading her to Jesus and the love of the Great Provider (see Matthew 6:26). I likewise want to lead that young man lost in the darkness of addiction to the Well of Life to quench his spiritual thirst with unending satisfaction (see John 4:14).

Jesus-like compassion will give us eyes to see the needs of others, and it will give us a desire that those with deep voids in their lives will find satisfaction in him. When I'm leading the Jesus way, I will be filled with compassion for the people in my community, my church, and within my influence so much that my heart will be burdened for them to the point of tears. I want to be the type of leader who is filled with the compassion of God so much that it drives me to tears.

As we become more like Jesus, the priorities in our ministries will center less on goals, strategies, and spreadsheets and more on prayers for the community, blessings for others, and love for our neighbors. May we consider others as those made in the image of God who need to know their Creator and his ways for them; may we see those we lead as more than volunteers, staff members, or numbers that make up our ministries. I pray that we will lead the Jesus way by looking at others with compassion.

Jesus Met Physical Needs

The needs we are most aware of are earthly needs. We're in tune with our bodies to know when we are tired. We notice when we are hungry. We know when it's time to get a haircut. We're aware when we are experiencing pain or sickness. Earthly needs are important because we *live* on this earth. Having our earthly needs met contributes to our physical, mental, and emotional well-being. One of the essential components of Jesus's leadership was that he showed a genuine concern for the earthly needs of others.

Meeting Needs by Healing

Perhaps the most prominent way we see this aspect of Jesus's leadership is in his healing others. I know there is a wide range of views on healings. Minimally, we should pray for people with physical needs, which is itself an act of mercy and compassion. However, some church leaders may practice more deliberate prayer for healing (laying on of hands, authoritative prayers, etc.). My intention is not to get into debate about how we should ask God to heal. My point is to acknowledge that Jesus cared about the physical health of others, and so should we.

Accounts of Jesus healing people fill the New Testament, with Jesus's care for people with physical infirmities on full display. For example, consider this man with leprosy who came to Jesus for healing:

> Large crowds followed Jesus as he came down the mountainside. Suddenly, a man with leprosy approached him and knelt before him. "Lord," the man said, "if you are willing, you can heal me and make me clean."

Jesus reached out and touched him. "I am willing," he said. "Be healed!" And instantly the leprosy disappeared. (Matthew 8:1–3)

We see that among all the crowds of people, this one man and his need mattered to Jesus. Jesus's compassion for people, particularly this man, moved him to action.

During another display of compassion, Jesus healed two blind men. Matthew says,

. . . two blind men followed along behind him, shouting, "Son of David, have mercy on us!"

They went right into the house where he was staying, and Jesus asked them, "Do you believe I can make you see?"

"Yes, Lord," they told him, "we do."

Then he touched their eyes and said, "Because of your faith, it will happen." Then their eyes were opened, and they could see! Jesus sternly warned them, "Don't tell anyone about this." But instead, they went out and spread his fame all over the region. (Matthew 9:27–31)

This story makes the compassion of Jesus obvious, doesn't it? The men cried out, "have mercy on us!" Mercy is what they needed, and *mercy* is exactly what Jesus showed them. People today also need mercy, yet I'm afraid that mercy is not very high on the list of qualities that many of today's leaders exhibit. Rather than leading by selfish motives, I want to lead as Jesus led—with mercy and compassion. I want to care about the physical well-being of others.

Meeting Needs by Feeding

Healing people was not the only way that Jesus displayed compassion for physical needs. There was a much more basic human need that Jesus addressed: hunger. A moment when Jesus met a major hunger need was the miracle of the feeding of the five thousand. This miracle is recorded in all four Gospels.

Jesus intended to get away to be alone with his disciples. However, as was often the case, wherever Jesus went, people followed. Mark's Gospel describes this display of compassion this way: "Jesus saw the huge crowd as he stepped from the boat, and he had compassion on them because they were like sheep without a shepherd. So he began teaching them many things" (Mark 6:34).

Jesus taught the people late into the afternoon. Realizing that folks were getting hungry, the disciples asked Jesus to send the people away to get some food. The disciples recognized the potential problem, but they didn't want to solve it. Jesus did. He not only had compassion on them because they were like sheep without a shepherd; he had compassion on them because they were hungry. Jesus would solve the physical need of the people. Mark says,

> Jesus took the five loaves and two fish, looked up toward heaven, and blessed them. Then, breaking the loaves into pieces, he kept giving the bread to the disciples so they could distribute it to the people. He also divided the fish for everyone to share. They all ate as much as they wanted, and afterward, the disciples picked up twelve baskets of leftover bread and fish. A total of 5,000 men and their families were fed. (Mark 6:41–44)

This story is not only miraculous, but it's also an incredible display of Jesus's heart toward people. Jesus intended to be alone with his disciples and teach them. However, they couldn't be alone. Wherever they went, people found them. Not only were these people encroaching on Jesus's time with his disciples, but they were also creating a logistical conundrum.

If you think thousands of people interrupting your plans would be a nuisance, think what it would be like if there were thousands of *hungry* people! Yet, Jesus wasn't angered or frustrated because of this problem. Instead, Jesus used this situation to teach his disciples, demonstrate his sovereign power, and display his compassion. Although the greater need of these people was spiritual in nature, Jesus didn't ignore their physical need.

As with Jesus, Jesus-like leaders not only see and meet physical needs themselves, but they should also teach others to see and meet physical needs. A few years ago, our church was really struggling. As a matter of fact, our church had begun to develop a negative reputation in the community. I knew that if we were going to become healthy again, we needed to "flip the script" concerning how our community viewed us. One of the ways we did this was through our food pantry ministry. God used our food pantry ministry in a simple yet powerful way to communicate to our community that we loved them. This ministry directly addressed the felt needs of people in our community and let them know that we love them.

A week before I wrote this chapter, our church showed our community how much we love them through our food pantry's Thanksgiving giveaway. We gave Thanksgiving food bags and gift cards to over 150 families in our community. As a task-oriented person, my natural desire would have been to stay in my office and work on my unending to-do list. After all, it was a Monday, and there was a lot to do. However, that is not how to lead the Jesus way.

So instead, I took time to visit with both our volunteers and over one hundred people from our community who gathered to experience the love of Jesus and his church. What a joy it was! I'm glad that God is changing my heart and making me more into a leader like Jesus. To this day, through dedicated donors and volunteers, our food pantry ministry continues to thrive and bless our community.

Prioritizing the Physical Needs of Others

We also see the compassion of Jesus when he frequently put others ahead of himself. We see his heart for others when he healed Simon Peter's mother-in-law. Luke tells us in Luke 4:38–39, "After leaving the synagogue that day, Jesus went to Simon's home, where he found Simon's mother-in-law very sick with a high fever. 'Please heal her,' everyone begged. Standing at her bedside, he rebuked the fever, and it left her. And she got up at once and prepared a meal for them."

You can almost hear the desperation of those present. "Please heal her," they said. If you read the previous verses from Luke 4, you can see that Jesus had already been teaching and casting out demons that day. He was probably quite tired. Take note of this: Jesus's concern for the needs of others outweighed his concern for his own needs. His heart for people led him to reprioritize his physical needs. He led by putting the needs of others ahead of his own.

Church leaders are busy, right? But we should never be too busy to love people. I should never be too busy and too focused on my desires or goals to lead the Jesus way. Answering emails, although important, is not more important than the person who sent the email. Spending time teaching a new believer how to read and study the Bible is more important than when I spend time reading the latest productivity book. Making sure that my staff knows that they are valued is more important than when I correct them for forgetting a task. We must prioritize people.

Consider another beautiful moment when Jesus prioritized someone, recorded in Luke 7:11–15. Luke tells us the story of a widow's only son. Let's pause for a moment to comprehend this situation. Not only had the woman's husband already died, but she had also lost her only son. Her son was likely the only one left who could take care of her. So, she was not only heartbroken, but she was also probably facing a future of helplessness. However, Jesus stepped in. Luke says,

> Soon afterward Jesus went with his disciples to the village of Nain, and a large crowd followed him. A funeral procession was coming out as he approached the village gate. The young man who had died was a widow's only son, and a large crowd from the village was with her. When the Lord saw her, his heart overflowed with compassion. "Don't cry!" he said. Then he walked over to the coffin and touched it, and the bearers stopped. "Young man," he said, "I tell you, get up." Then the dead boy sat up and began to talk! And Jesus gave him back to his mother.

Notice Luke's description: Jesus's heart "overflowed with compassion." To lead the Jesus way, we must understand the importance of the physical needs of people. The people within our influence don't need more leaders who lead in worldly ways. They need more leaders who lead the Jesus way.

In each of these situations, Jesus could have easily said he was too busy to address these earthly needs. He could have said that he had other priorities. After all, the primary mission of Jesus was spiritual, not earthly. Yet, that wasn't how Jesus reacted to these needs. He recognized needs. He had time. He had concern. He had compassion. A leader like Jesus must be alert and sensitive to people's earthly needs. He or she must prioritize these needs as an integral part of his or her ministry and leadership.

To lead like Jesus, you will need to discover how you can best meet earthly needs in your context. Perhaps you can go on a mission trip to love others in the name of Jesus by building homes, installing water wells, or conducting a medical clinic. Perhaps you can serve those in your community by developing a clothing closet ministry or providing after-school care to children and families. Look for possibilities of how you can be a leader who meets the needs of others and who leads others to meet needs. Be creative, purposeful, and prayerful as God works through you.

Jesus Met Spiritual Needs

Although Jesus was concerned with earthly needs, he was primarily tuned in to and concerned with people's spiritual needs. Therefore, if you want to lead the Jesus way, you will also seek to be in tune with the spiritual needs of those around you.

The spiritual concern that Jesus had for others stemmed from his very nature as the Son of God. The spiritual compassion of Jesus toward those he encountered mirrors the compassion that God the Father has toward all those created in his image. This compassion was fully displayed when Jesus taught one of his most famous parables: the parable of the lost sheep. Jesus offered this parable in Matthew 18:12–14:

If a man has a hundred sheep and one of them wanders away, what will he do? Won't he leave the ninety-nine others on the hills and go out to search for the one that is lost? And if he finds it, I tell you the truth, he will rejoice over it more than over the ninety-nine that didn't wander away! In the same way, it is not my heavenly Father's will that even one of these little ones should perish.

God's will is that not even one of those precious to him will perish. It should also be the will of those who lead the Jesus way that not one of those within our influence should feel lost, confused, or helpless in his or her spiritual life.

We should be willing to give extra effort to rescue those who have wandered spiritually. We should make the additional phone call or visit to bring clarity to those who are spiritually confused. We should be willing to spend more time in prayer on behalf of that nomadic soul. We should be more like Jesus and we should minister as Jesus ministered.

Jesus Called People out of Darkness

Jesus-driven leaders must also be keenly aware that many people live in spiritual darkness. Those we encounter may experience confusion, depression, fear, discouragement, anger, or addiction resulting from evil spiritual attacks in their lives. Jesus was aware of spiritual darkness and addressed it head-on in his ministry.

The story of Jesus healing a boy who was tormented by demon possession offers a vivid example of Jesus coming face-to-face with spiritual darkness. Luke describes this moment in Luke 9:37–43:

The next day, after they had come down the mountain, a large crowd met Jesus. A man in the crowd called out to him, "Teacher, I beg you to look at my son, my only child. An evil spirit keeps seizing him, making him scream. It throws him into convulsions so that he foams at the mouth. It batters him and hardly ever leaves him alone. I begged your disciples to cast out the spirit, but they couldn't do it."

Jesus said, "You faithless and corrupt people! How long must I be with you and put up with you?" Then he said to the man, "Bring your son here."

As the boy came forward, the demon knocked him to the ground and threw him into a violent convulsion. But Jesus rebuked the evil spirit and healed the boy. Then he gave him back to his father. Awe gripped the people as they saw this majestic display of God's power.

To be sure, there isn't a clear consensus about the relationship between Christian ministry and demon possession in today's church. However, there should be consensus about this: ministry leaders should have a deep and compassionate concern for those in spiritual darkness.

To lead the Jesus way means that we will take those who are spiritually oppressed to the only one who has the power to help them: Jesus. Leading the Jesus way means that we are certain these people know the story of Jesus and the power of his resurrection. It means we pray for these people and teach them the power of prayer. It means we point them to passages of Scripture that demonstrate God's power over darkness and sin. To lead the Jesus way means that we will seek to bring spiritual light into the hearts, minds, and lives of those oppressed by evil.

Jesus Called People to Repentance

Being rescued from our sin is the most significant spiritual need for each of us. Jesus regularly met this need by calling people to repentance. Jesus understood better than anyone how desperately people need to experience communion with God. Every human needs to turn from sin and turn to God. To lead the Jesus way means to compassionately call people to repentance.

Jesus was calling people to repent of their sins from the beginning of his ministry. Before calling his disciples to follow him, he was calling for repentance. Matthew 4:17 tells us, "From then on Jesus began to preach, 'Repent of your sins and turn to God, for the Kingdom of Heaven is near.'" In John 8:11 Jesus said to a woman caught in adultery, "Go and sin no more." The call to spiritual transformation was not an occasional act for Jesus; it was at the heart of Jesus's ministry and leadership.

Recently, I introduced myself as a pastor to a woman in a convenience store. She immediately started sharing with me some physical needs that she had. Although her physical needs mattered, I sensed from the Holy Spirit that this lady needed to hear that what she most needed was Jesus himself. Her spiritual need was the greatest need she had. I told her that our church would consider helping her with some of her needs, but more than anything else, we could give her the love of Jesus.

Leaders who lead the Jesus way realize that showing compassion doesn't mean we overlook sins. We must take seriously what the apostle Paul said in Romans 6:23, "the wages of sin is death," and Romans 3:23, "everyone has sinned; we all fall short of God's glorious standard." Sin is deadly. Leading with compassion means lovingly and clearly pointing those we lead to repentance. Leading with compassion means leading others to Jesus and his great atonement. As Paul beautifully concludes in Romans 6:23, " . . . but the free gift of God is eternal life through Christ Jesus our Lord."

Even now you can pray for those who are on your mind who are suffering in some spiritual way. As a spiritual leader, you must care about the spiritual needs of others. Take spiritual needs seriously, and take those needs to Jesus.

Jesus Met Needs with Gentleness and Patience

"Don't pray for patience because God might just give it to you." I've heard that statement many times over the years. I realize the hesitancy some may have in praying for patience. They know that God often develops patience in our lives by allowing us to endure difficult circumstances. However, we should welcome the opportunity to be more like Jesus. We should want to become the people God created and called us to be. I've learned that to lead the Jesus way, I must pray for and develop patience and gentleness in my life.

Jesus certainly had patience with those closest to him—a patience that we don't always show toward others. We're probably too harsh in our judgment of the early disciples of Jesus, in fact. After all, it's easy to say what we would do if we were in their shoes now that we're reflecting upon the events two thousand years later. The disciples didn't transition from ordinary people to world-changing apostles overnight. They often grumbled with one another, fought against the plans of Jesus, misunderstood his teaching, and prioritized the ways of the world over the ways of God. Even for them, though, Jesus was a model of patience and grace.

Gentleness and Patience with Martha

You may remember the story of Mary and Martha from chapter 1, where we looked at how Jesus displayed gentleness and compassion toward one of these sisters. Luke tells us a story of Jesus visiting their home in Luke 10:38–42:

> As Jesus and the disciples continued on their way to Jerusalem, they came to a certain village where a woman named Martha welcomed him into her home. Her sister, Mary, sat at the Lord's feet, listening to what he taught. But Martha was distracted by the big dinner she was preparing. She came to Jesus and said, "Lord, doesn't it seem unfair to you that my sister just sits here while I do all the work? Tell her to come and help me."
>
> But the Lord said to her, "My dear Martha, you are worried and upset over all these details! There is only one thing worth being concerned about. Mary has discovered it, and it will not be taken away from her."

To be honest, I can identify with Martha in this story. After all, she was the one who welcomed Jesus, yet she is not able to spend time with Jesus because her sister is not helping with the household work that comes along with having a guest. However, we must pay attention to these words because they are key to understanding this story: "But Martha was distracted by the big dinner she was preparing." Dinner is great, but the priority was Jesus, not dinner. Martha's priorities were misaligned.

Sometimes, those we lead will also have their priorities out of alignment, but listen to how Jesus responded to Martha: "My dear Martha. . . ." Jesus didn't harshly rebuke her; he lovingly corrected her and steered her back to himself. Leading the Jesus way requires being patient and gentle as we help our followers see godly priorities.

Sometimes it may baffle us when those we lead seem so off-target. You may wonder if they will ever understand what you are trying to teach them. Perhaps a deacon in your church is pushing other church members in a direction that goes against the church's vision. Perhaps you are mentoring someone to be a better Bible teacher, and they seem to be ignoring all the advice you are pouring into them. Perhaps that new staff member seems hopeless when it comes to completing necessary functions of the job. Be like Jesus; be patient and gentle. Loving redirection will be a crucial tool in your Jesus-like leadership toolbox.

Gentleness and Patience with Mary Magdalene

Another example of Jesus displaying patience and gentleness involves a different Mary. Mary Magdalene was downcast and distraught after Jesus's crucifixion. She had lost her Lord and teacher. She was so deep in despair that she didn't even realize Jesus had risen from the dead and was standing in her midst. John tells us about an exchange between Jesus and Mary in John 20:11–18:

> Mary was standing outside the tomb crying, and as she wept, she stooped and looked in. She saw two white-robed angels, one sitting at the head and the other at the foot of the place where the body of Jesus had been lying. "Dear woman, why are you crying?" the angels asked her.
>
> "Because they have taken away my Lord," she replied, "and I don't know where they have put him."

She turned to leave and saw someone standing there. It was Jesus, but she didn't recognize him. "Dear woman, why are you crying?" Jesus asked her. "Who are you looking for?"

She thought he was the gardener. "Sir," she said, "if you have taken him away, tell me where you have put him, and I will go and get him."

"Mary!" Jesus said.

She turned to him and cried out, "Rabboni!" (which is Hebrew for "Teacher").

Jesus was patient and caring with Mary. He could have easily stated, "Mary, I can't believe you don't even recognize me! You thought I was the gardener? Really?" However, Jesus does not respond that way to those he loves. Instead, he was patient and kind with Mary. He lovingly guided her back to himself. Once again, we see loving and gentle correction. Jesus was patient with Mary and gave her time to take in all that was happening. He gave her a chance to comprehend that he, her Lord, was speaking to her.

Gentleness and Patience with Thomas

Jesus showed patience to the twelve apostles as well. One particular disciple who required some patience was Thomas, "the Twin." Nowadays Thomas has another nickname, "Doubting Thomas," because he didn't always accept things right away. Jesus had to be patient with Thomas.

I resonate with Thomas sometimes, though I prefer to call him "Confirming Thomas." I feel that Thomas simply wanted to confirm things before he believed them. His most famous story of wanting to confirm something is when he was told that Jesus had risen from the dead. Listen to how the Bible describes this moment:

One of the twelve disciples, Thomas (nicknamed the Twin), was not with the others when Jesus came. They told him, "We have seen the Lord!"

But he replied, "I won't believe it unless I see the nail wounds in his hands, put my fingers into them, and place my hand into the wound in his side."

Eight days later the disciples were together again, and this time Thomas was with them. The doors were locked; but suddenly, as before, Jesus was standing among them. "Peace be with you," he said. Then he said to Thomas, "Put your finger here, and look at my hands. Put your hand into the wound in my side. Don't be faithless any longer. Believe!"

"My Lord and my God!" Thomas exclaimed.

Then Jesus told him, "You believe because you have seen me. Blessed are those who believe without seeing me." (John 20:24-29)

Again, Jesus is patient and kind. Jesus didn't mention that several others had already reported that he had risen from the dead and perhaps Thomas should trust them. He didn't remind Thomas that he told the disciples repeatedly that he would rise from the dead. Jesus simply provided the evidence Thomas needed so he would believe. Jesus was loving and gentle.

We may encounter someone who needs a little more time to come to an understanding of the truth. Those we lead may initially push back against what we are teaching them or leading them toward. They may be downright difficult sometimes. Leading with the compassion of Jesus requires Christlike tolerance and love with those who need more time to be transformed into godly followers of Jesus. A little more patience and gentleness may be precisely what they need to continue to develop into who God has called them to be.

When you're feeling impatient with others, remind yourself to fight to be a Jesus-like leader. Focus on taking a breath (my Apple Watch even has an app that helps me breathe and relax). Say a short prayer, and ask God's Spirit to give you supernatural peace and patience. Remind yourself how patient God has been with you in your spiritual life. These steps will help you be kind and gentle with those you lead, as Jesus was.

Gentleness and Patience according to Paul

Before leaving this discussion of the patience and gentleness of Jesus, it's worth noting what the apostle Paul had to say about these two Christian attributes. When describing the evidence of the Holy Spirit in the lives of believers, Paul says in Galatians 5:22–23, "But the Holy Spirit produces this kind of fruit in our lives: love, joy, peace, patience, kindness, goodness, faithfulness, gentleness, and self-control. There is no law against these things!"

Did you see the words? Among the qualities listed as fruit of the Holy Spirit are *patience* and *gentleness*. Elsewhere, Paul describes the characteristics of love (the ultimate Christian virtue):

> Love is patient and kind. Love is not jealous or boastful or proud or rude. It does not demand its own way. It is not irritable, and it keeps no record of being wronged. It does not rejoice about injustice but rejoices whenever the truth wins out. Love never gives up, never loses faith, is always hopeful, and endures through every circumstance. (1 Corinthians 13:4–7)

To show true, godly love, you must possess patience and kindness. To lead the Jesus way, you must have compassion-driven patience and gentleness for those you lead.

I can quickly think of multiple times when I was impatient or unkind. I'm not proud of these moments. I don't want to be an impatient and unkind leader; I want to lead the Jesus way. Leading like Jesus means displaying qualities that are evidence of the Holy Spirit in your life and leadership. Leading the Jesus way means loving others with the kind of love that Jesus has. You can do it; you can lead the Jesus way by seeing and meeting needs with patience and gentleness.

Conclusion

As you seek to lead people, you're going to see that they have a variety of needs. Those needs are obvious at times. At other times, they will be hidden below the surface. To lead the Jesus way means to be sensitive and responsive to the needs of those you lead.

Although Jesus is still changing me, I'm much better at seeing and meeting needs than I used to be. God has used specific experiences (like the one I described in this chapter's introduction with the woman who got news of her disease) to draw me closer to him and his ways. These experiences have made me more like Jesus. Of course, I still struggle from time to time in being sensitive to needs, and so will you. However, as we grow to be more like Jesus, we can recognize those moments, correct them, learn from them, and lead more like Jesus.

Jesus was a compassionate leader. Will you examine yourself to consider how God might grow you into a compassionate leader?

The second guidepost of leaders who lead the Jesus way is to see and meet needs. Part of how we care for people is to teach them about Jesus and his ways. That's the topic of the next chapter, so let's continue to discover how to lead the Jesus way.

Key Takeaways from This Chapter

1. Jesus led by displaying compassionate care.
2. Jesus led by caring for physical needs.
3. Jesus led by caring for spiritual needs.
4. Jesus led by being gentle and patient.

Action Steps for Leaders

1. Reflect and journal about how you can lead by being more compassionate.
2. Identify three ways you can meet the needs of others each week.
3. Write the word "compassion" somewhere that will remind you to lead like Jesus.
4. Ask someone you trust to remind you when you are being impatient or ungentle.

3
Leading through Teaching

SUZANNE DIRECTS THE SMALL GROUP MINISTRY at her church, Ravenhead United Methodist Church. Suzanne grew up in the church and has been serving as a volunteer since she was in college. However, a lot has changed for the church in the last few years, including an explosion of growth. Now in her early forties, Suzanne is one of the highest-level volunteers in the church.

Ravenhead UMC has added many new small groups due to the church's rapid growth. The challenge is most of the leaders of those small groups don't have much experience leading a small group. Suzanne's task is to lead them, and she's up for the task. At least, she thought she was.

Suzanne has encountered a tremendous amount of frustration. She has told the small group leaders to stick to the lesson and not get side-tracked on nuanced theological issues and political hot topics. But as Suzanne sits in some groups, she notices that some leaders have rejected her guidance. She's encouraged the group leaders to empower other group members to serve in various ways. Yet, she still sees the leaders overburdening themselves by doing everything on their own. It seems as if the group leaders just don't know what they're doing. But then Suzanne realizes that is precisely the problem. To lead these small group leaders, Suzanne needs to *teach* them what to do; she can't just tell them what to do.

At first thought, some may not consider teaching an ingredient of leadership. However, teaching is integral to leadership. Imagine trying to lead someone to become a more faithful follower of God without teaching them the ways of God. That doesn't make any sense. When leading people, we must tell them, show them, and teach them which direction they must go. Leaders must teach followers before they can follow well.

I'm thankful for those who taught me in my early days of ministry. I remember the first time I went on a hospital visit as a ministry intern. A seasoned minister told me to meet him at the church to join him on a ministry visit to one of the local hospitals. I had no idea what I was doing, and I was uncomfortable. He walked me through the process and showed me some tips along the way. He taught me the best place to park, what to say and what not to say to the patient, why I should wash my hands before and after the visit, and so much more. The helpful advice he provided gave me the confidence to carry out this critical ministry task.

No one was better at teaching others than Jesus. His teaching ministry was foundational to his leadership. I've learned that to lead the Jesus way, I must learn to teach the Jesus way.

Jesus Taught with Wisdom

As we explore the teaching ministry of Jesus, we need to realize that Jesus was not just a teacher; he was a *wise* teacher. He wasn't trying to help people become intelligent; he was trying to help them grow in wisdom. To lead the Jesus way, we must not only develop wisdom ourselves, but we must also teach others how they can build wisdom.

The New Testament Gospels are a treasure house full of Jesus's wisdom. He displayed wisdom when the religious leaders tried to back him into a corner or catch him in an intellectual trap. Time and again they failed to do so. For instance, there was the time the religious leaders claimed Jesus cast out demons by the power of demons. Listen to the wise response of Jesus:

Any kingdom divided by civil war is doomed. A family splintered by feuding will fall apart. You say I am empowered by Satan. But if Satan is divided and fighting against himself, how can his kingdom survive? And if I am empowered by Satan, what about your own exorcists? They cast out demons, too, so they will condemn you for what you have said. But if I am casting out demons by the power of God, then the Kingdom of God has arrived among you. For when a strong man is fully armed and guards his palace, his possessions are safe— until someone even stronger attacks and overpowers him, strips him of his weapons, and carries off his belongings.

Anyone who isn't with me opposes me, and anyone who isn't working with me is actually working against me. (Luke 11:17–23)

Jesus pointed out the logical inconsistency in the religious leaders' claims. I can't help but smile when I hear Jesus respond this way. Surely, the religious leaders did not anticipate this response. Likely, they were unaccustomed to that level of wisdom. Jesus didn't merely address the accusation against him; he was teaching as he was responding.

Jesus was challenged on another occasion. This time it had to do with paying taxes to Caesar. Again, Jesus responded with divine wisdom (see Matthew 17:24–27). Jesus was intentional not to undermine the authority of Caesar, while at the same time he did not endorse Caesar. Jesus was so wise. Of course, the wisdom of Jesus was godly wisdom. As Jesus taught, his supernatural wisdom often attracted others to want to learn more from him (see Matthew 7:9 and John 4:29). Those who wanted wisdom knew they could find it with Jesus. Genuine wisdom is attractive. This reality should drive church leaders to develop and dispense wisdom.

Mark 12:35–37 describes another moment when those who sought wisdom found it with Jesus. Verse 37 says, "The large crowd listened to him with great delight." Pay attention to that last phrase: They listened to Jesus with "great delight." The people responded with delight to the wisdom of Jesus. If the people we lead are exposed to godly wisdom, they will want more. They're going to take great delight in it. So let's give them more.

You and I must be filled with the truth of God so that we lead as Jesus led. Here are some ways that we can be filled with God's truth: We must pray that the Holy Spirit will give us divine wisdom. You can challenge yourself to become a wiser leader by making an appointment with someone who displays godly wisdom and asking how they developed into who they are. I can read one chapter of the book of Proverbs every day and seek to glean wisdom. I can be a wise leader, and so can you. We don't have to accept the status quo. We can be teaching-leaders who are filled with godly wisdom, as Jesus was.

Jesus Taught Large Groups

Every time Jesus taught, he taught with a specific context, in a specific setting, at a specific time. Each moment was unique. One aspect that made these settings distinct was the size of the group Jesus taught. Jesus sometimes taught one-on-one, he sometimes taught in small groups, and he sometimes taught in large groups—which is the focus of this section.

When I say "large groups," I don't mean fifty or a hundred. Sometimes, Jesus taught *thousands* of people at a time. Remember the feeding of the five thousand back in chapter 2? Well, the people Jesus fed were hungry for a reason. They had stayed late into the afternoon listening to Jesus teach. Remember, Mark tells us in Mark 6:34, "Jesus saw the huge crowd as he stepped from the boat, and he had compassion on them because they were like sheep without a shepherd. So he began *teaching* them many things."

This group of five thousand wasn't the only large crowd that gathered to hear Jesus teach. Mark tells us in 8:1, "About this time another large crowd had gathered, and the people ran out of food again." We learn that this second crowd numbered four thousand men. Luke tells us that crowds also gathered at the temple to hear Jesus. He says, "Every day Jesus went to the Temple to teach, and each evening he returned to spend the night on the Mount of Olives. The crowds gathered at the Temple early each morning to hear him" (Luke 21:37–38). Teaching crowds was not something Jesus occasionally did; it was a repeated occurrence for him.

Once, on a mission trip to Brazil, I had firsthand experience teaching various group sizes. In one setting, I was speaking one-on-one with someone about Jesus. In another location, I was sharing with ten to twenty people what God had done in my life. Then, I taught a group of over five hundred people. That one was memorable. I'll never forget when I was given short notice that I would speak to a group of over five hundred former criminals. I was a young man who had never spoken to a group that large, particularly a group of former criminals who didn't speak my native language. I learned quickly I must always be prepared to teach as Jesus taught, no matter the size of the group.

I've learned that leading like Jesus means that I am prepared to teach in any ministry context. I've learned to prepare by being immersed in God's Word and exposed to the godly wisdom of others. We can prepare to be adaptable teachers by regular Bible reading, careful reflection and thought, continual discussion of God's truth with other wise and godly learners, and frequent practice.

Church leaders will encounter opportunities to teach large crowds. As Jesus did, we may have the opportunity to teach dozens, hundreds, or even thousands at a time. No matter how large the group is, we must seize the opportunity. We must realize that God has given us the chance to lead like Jesus by sharing with many people all that God has done.

Jesus Taught Small Groups

Jesus was also a master of teaching small groups. The bulk of his small-group teaching took place with those who spent every day with him: the twelve apostles. Jesus was continually teaching the disciples while they shared their lives together. Sometimes, Jesus encouraged them through his teaching. Sometimes he corrected them. At other times Jesus enlightened them as he taught. In any manner, Jesus was always intentional when he taught. He took advantage of these small-group settings as a time to be focused and purposeful with just a few people.

The small-group nature allowed the disciples to ask Jesus questions. These settings were laboratories for wisdom. For example, in Luke 11 we observe the disciples asking Jesus to help them pray, and Jesus gladly helps them.

Once Jesus was in a certain place praying. As he finished, one of his disciples came to him and said, "Lord, teach us to pray, just as John taught his disciples."

Jesus said, "This is how you should pray: Father, may your name be kept holy. May your Kingdom come soon. Give us each day the food we need, and forgive us our sins, as we forgive those who sin against us. And don't let us yield to temptation." (Luke 11:1–4)

This moment was ideal for Jesus to thrive as a teacher. Consider how important prayer is and how valuable this opportunity was for Jesus to teach his followers—and for his followers to learn from him. Just as Jesus did, we must recognize that small groups are prime opportunities for teaching, and we must seize the moment to teach as Jesus taught.

Sometimes, a small group can be as few as two or three people. With Jesus, this was often Peter, James, and John. They went with Jesus to particular places and witnessed miracles that the other disciples did not encounter (see Matthew 17:1–13). Mark 5:37 tells us of a moment when Jesus chose only Peter, James, and John to join him for a miracle. Mark says, "Then Jesus stopped the crowd and wouldn't let anyone go with him except Peter, James, and John (the brother of James)." On this occasion, these three witnessed Jesus miraculously bring a dead girl back to life (see Mark 5:38–43). We don't know precisely why he did it, but we know that Jesus had a reason to take just these three.

On another occasion, Jesus took the three with him when he was radiantly transfigured before them (see Mark 9:2–3). At yet another time, Jesus took this inner circle of disciples to pray with him just before his crucifixion (see Matthew 26:36–38). Think about these three momentous encounters that Jesus shared with Peter, James, and John: the raising of a girl from the dead, the transfiguration of Jesus, and the special prayer time with Jesus before he gave his life on the cross. Jesus was intentional with his investment in these three; he had them with him on purpose. Because they experienced exclusive opportunities with Jesus, they could also learn unique lessons from Jesus. God would go on to use Peter, James, and John as monumental figures in the life of the early church.

I've discovered over the years that I can influence an intentionally small group of people in a specific and special way. I currently have a discipleship group that meets weekly for Bible study and personal development. I know these men more deeply, and they know me deeper than others do. Nearly twenty years ago when I was youth minister, I chose three sixth grade boys to meet with on Sunday afternoons. I couldn't meet with every young man in our youth ministry, but I could meet with them. I still have a lasting relationship with those men, who are now husbands and fathers. I've found that I can have much more concentrated impact on a small group than on a large group. I can lead like Jesus in this way, and so can you.

Jesus Taught One-on-One

Experienced leaders know that their most incredible teaching opportunities often come in a one-on-one context. After all, some of the most famous teacher-student relationships in popular culture (even the fictional ones) are one-on-one relationships. Consider Yoda and Luke Skywalker in the Star Wars films. Or the special relationship between Harry and Professor Dumbledore in the Harry Potter book series. Elijah and Elisha shared this relationship as Old Testament prophets (see 1 Kings 19 and 2 Kings 2). The apostle Paul shared this relationship with Timothy and Titus as he developed them as young pastors (see 1 Timothy, 2 Timothy, and Titus). There's something special about the teacher-student relationship.

The life of Jesus also included one-on-one teaching relationships. Peter was often the beneficiary of these one-on-one lessons, though his learning frequently came in the form of correction (Peter was good at letting his mouth get him into trouble). After Jesus had risen from the dead, he took one such moment to prepare Peter for the tremendous ministry that awaited him.

After breakfast Jesus asked Simon Peter, "Simon son of John, do you love me more than these?"

"Yes, Lord," Peter replied, "you know I love you."

"Then feed my lambs," Jesus told him.

Jesus repeated the question: "Simon son of John, do you love me?"

"Yes, Lord," Peter said, "you know I love you."

"Then take care of my sheep," Jesus said.

A third time he asked him, "Simon son of John, do you love me?"

Peter was hurt that Jesus asked the question a third time. He said, "Lord, you know everything. You know that I love you."

Jesus said, "Then feed my sheep". (John 21:15–17)

John points out that Peter was hurt when Jesus continued asking him the same question. This moment was likely difficult for Peter. He had denied Jesus *three times* before Jesus was crucified. Now, Jesus asked Peter *three times* if he loved him. Surely Peter was still recovering from the guilt of his denial of Jesus. It probably felt like salt poured into his emotional wound.

Jesus went on in John 21 to tell Peter how God would use him in the future. However, perhaps the most crucial aspect of this moment was that Jesus used it to teach Peter about forgiveness and restoration. Jesus's method with Peter involved one-on-one interaction, allowing Peter to fail and grow, and following up by reinforcing what he wanted Peter to learn. This method was much more effective than something that might have occurred in a classroom. Rather than Peter retreating in shame and despair, Jesus commissioned him to lead with boldness and power. Peter went through a lot with Jesus (good and bad). Consequently, Peter had great opportunities to learn. The personal investment Jesus made into Peter would invigorate Peter for ministry, and that investment would ignite a spark that helped set the early church ablaze.

As with Jesus and Peter, sometimes the opportunities to teach may be as small as just one individual. We must recognize these exceptional teaching opportunities. God can use those moments as a catalyst in the life of someone on the brink of failure or despair. He can also use these moments to impact the lives of others for generations to come.

Whether it's one, three, twelve, or somewhere in between, we must recognize that leading the Jesus way means being able to teach small groups. Sometimes we forget the necessity of teaching in small groups. Don't fall into that trap. Be intentional. Take some time to prepare a few of your deacons on how they can better minister to homebound members of your church. Take your greeters to meet with the first impressions director at a church that is thriving at welcoming guests. Spend extra time with your core ministry team and teach them how to empower others through encouragement and healthy accountability.

Sometimes God will do more through you teaching a small group than through you teaching hundreds or even thousands. The concentrated impact of your leadership in the lives of just a few may have compounding results that unfold for years to come. You can lead the Jesus way by embracing the work of teaching small groups.

Jesus Sometimes Taught in Simple Ways

Effective teachers can teach profound truths in simple ways. Jesus was an expert at teaching simply. The most famous method Jesus used to teach simply was through parables. Parables are earthly stories that communicate a heavenly truth. To lead like Jesus, you will certainly need to share heavenly truth. So, learn from the Master. Pay attention to how Jesus taught sacred truth in a way that those on earth could understand.

Let's reflect on some of the most famous parables of Jesus. First, consider once again the parable of the lost sheep (see Luke 15:1–7). This parable is a simple story that explains God the Father's loving concern for one lost sinner—a wonderful truth, simply and masterfully communicated. Or take the parable of the soils (see Mark 4:1–20). Again, Jesus used a simple story about dirt, birds, thorns, a path, and seeds to explain how the truth of the gospel takes root in the hearts of some but not in the hearts of others. Some of us are so familiar with these parables that we forget how simple yet powerful they are. None of us is able to teach parables as Jesus did, but as I lead God's people, I can and must learn how to take heavenly truths and communicate them in a way that is simple to understand.

If you consider *all* the principles, laws, and instructions in the Bible, you may be overwhelmed by the sheer volume. However, Jesus waded through the complexity of the Bible's teachings and simply communicated to his followers how to understand what was most important about God's ways. Matthew tells us about this fantastic display of simple, effective teaching in Matthew 22:34–40:

> But when the Pharisees heard that he had silenced the Sadducees with his reply, they met together to question him again. One of them, an expert in religious law, tried to trap him with this question: "Teacher, which is the most important commandment in the law of Moses?"
>
> Jesus replied, "'You must love the Lord your God with all your heart, all your soul, and all your mind.' This is the first and greatest commandment. A second is equally important: 'Love your neighbor as yourself.' The entire law and all the demands of the prophets are based on these two commandments."

The one who questioned Jesus was "an expert in religious law." Yet, Jesus schooled the expert by simplifying what the "experts" had made complex.

At times, those under our influence will be eager to learn the ways of God. Leading the Jesus way means teaching these great truths in simple ways. It's helpful to ask questions such as, "What is the most important piece of truth to learn from this teaching? How can I teach this truth in a way that compares to something my hearers already understand? If I had to teach this lesson in thirty seconds, how would I teach it?"

There will also be times as a leader when you may feel like those you lead don't understand what you are teaching them. They may need a simple explanation to bring clarity. Jesus faced this challenge as well. On one occasion, Jesus addressed a question regarding his teaching with a simple truth he revealed through a story. We know this story as the story of the good Samaritan (see Luke 10:30–37). A question was raised as to how to love a neighbor. The straightforward yet effective teaching strategy Jesus used in this story revealed the unavoidable truth: the Samaritan was the one who loved as a neighbor should love. Jesus very simply replied, "now go and do the same."

As the Lord has grown my teaching abilities, I have learned that sometimes the best way to teach is to teach simply. When I was in seminary, I fell so in love with teaching God's Word that I felt I had to teach every angle of every interpretation of the biblical text. Then, I realized that if I say too much, my people won't hear anything I say. So, in recent years, when I preach a sermon, I boil the sermon down to a "bottom line," which is one simple statement that summarizes the biblical teaching. Before we dismiss the worship service, I give our people "weekly challenges," which are simple steps they can take to live out what they learned from the Bible. For example, regarding the parable of the lost sheep, I might say, "The bottom line is that Jesus cares about every lost soul." Then, I may challenge our people to identify one lost person to pray for and seek opportunity to share the gospel with them. Having grown as a teacher, I now seek to teach biblical truth in a way that is simple and powerful rather than sharing everything that has ever been said about a passage.

If we're going to lead like Jesus, we must work to master the art of teaching in a simple way. Our leadership will blossom once we develop the ability to understand God's ways and teach them in a simple way.

Jesus Sometimes Taught in More Complex Ways

Although Jesus often taught in a simple way, there were times that he chose to teach in a way that may have initially been challenging for his learners to grasp. Likewise, there will be times for those who lead like Jesus to use this same methodology. You may want to teach a new principle that stretches the minds of those you lead. Maybe you're trying to teach something pertinent to a particular group of people but not others. Occasionally, you'll want to present a truth that gives the learner something to ponder. These are all scenarios that Jesus encountered as he taught others.

To be clear, we are not to teach in a complex way merely for the sake of complexity. That is not leading the Jesus way. We should not seek to show how brilliant we are, how many hours of study we put in, or how many confusing analogies we can use. This was not why Jesus taught in complex ways. Rather, he always had an end goal to bring the learner back to understanding his words and God's ways.

Consider how Jesus taught the biblical principle of being "born again" in a way that was initially complex to the one he taught. Today, followers of Jesus use the phrase "born again" quite often. Most reading this book probably know that this phrase means that someone is made new by the power of the gospel of Jesus. To modern Christians, *born again* is an elementary phrase. However, that was not always the case.

For example, there was a man named Nicodemus, a Jewish leader who was quite educated, yet the phrase "born again" was too complex for him to grasp. Notice this interaction between Jesus and Nicodemus:

There was a man named Nicodemus, a Jewish religious leader who was a Pharisee. After dark one evening, he came to speak with Jesus. "Rabbi," he said, "we all know that God has sent you to teach us. Your miraculous signs are evidence that God is with you."

Jesus replied, "I tell you the truth, unless you are born again, you cannot see the Kingdom of God."

"What do you mean?" exclaimed Nicodemus. "How can an old man go back into his mother's womb and be born again?"

Jesus replied, "I assure you, no one can enter the Kingdom of God without being born of water and the Spirit. Humans can reproduce only human life, but the Holy Spirit gives birth to spiritual life. So don't be surprised when I say, 'You must be born again.' The wind blows wherever it wants. Just as you can hear the wind but can't tell where it comes from or where it is going, so you can't explain how people are born of the Spirit."

"How are these things possible?" Nicodemus asked.

Jesus replied, "You are a respected Jewish teacher, and yet you don't understand these things?" (John 3:1–10)

This interaction between Jesus and Nicodemus is fascinating. Nicodemus' confusion was on full display when he replied, "How are these things possible?" Jesus knew this concept was complex to Nicodemus, yet he presented it to Nicodemus anyway. He had a purpose in teaching this way: to press Nicodemus in his heart and mind to move beyond all he thought he knew about God to really discover what was most important in faithfulness to God. He would introduce a truth to Nicodemus that would later be understood by a small child who gave their life to Jesus. Yet, at that time, this truth was totally missed by a highly educated Jewish teacher.

In the next chapter of John's Gospel, we are told of another interaction Jesus had with someone where he spoke in a way she didn't understand at first. The story of the Samaritan woman at the well is a beautiful picture of how Jesus walked someone from a complex statement to an explicit declaration of God's truth. In an exchange where Jesus asks the woman for water, he was able to teach her something powerful about how he is the living water (see John 4:26).

Jesus offered the woman that living water, but she couldn't even figure how Jesus could drink water without a bucket. But Jesus didn't jump straight to the point. He allowed her not to understand as he built a beautiful bridge to bear the truth that he was about to share with her. Jesus said, "Anyone who drinks this water will soon become thirsty again. But those who drink the water I give will never be thirsty again. It becomes a fresh, bubbling spring within them, giving them eternal life" (John 4:14). The woman began to recognize that Jesus was speaking of spiritual realities, so she transitioned to talk of spiritual things—including the idea that a Messiah would come. Finally, Jesus hit her with the wonderful reality that *he* is that Messiah.

This woman was at first utterly perplexed about what Jesus was saying when their conversation began. She was thinking only about physical and concrete realities (i.e., actual water). Jesus used something that was complex at first to move to a powerful spiritual moment; he moved from the abstract image of living water to the truth that he was the giver of life. As he did with this woman, Jesus would sometimes wait to unveil what he was teaching until spiritual eyes and hearts were opened enough to understand his truth.

By witnessing the model of Jesus, I've learned that using more complex ways of teaching may be right at times. For example, as church leaders, we must master the skills of asking questions that stretch the minds of others. We might ask them, "What principles of evangelism do we learn by comparing and contrasting the stories of Nicodemus and the woman at the well?" We must also discover how to build on, clarify, and apply foundational truths already in the minds of those we lead. An example for us may be to ask those we lead to prove biblically that even the person who has never heard the gospel is still lost without Christ. To lead like Jesus, we must help those within our influence realize and embrace the deep truths of God, even when it requires using complex teaching methods to get them there.

On the other hand, we also need to realize that the complex teachings of Jesus were sometimes offensive to those who heard them. In one example, some of those who heard Jesus were even confused in thinking that he was advocating cannibalism (see John 6:47–60). Jesus said, "Anyone who eats the bread from heaven, however, will never die. I am the living bread that came down from heaven. Anyone who eats this bread will live forever; and this bread, which I will offer so the world may live, is my flesh" (vv. 50–51). The people's response showed their confusion: "How can this man give us his flesh to eat?" (v. 52).

If Jesus were concerned with keeping the teaching simple, this would have been the time to clarify what he was saying. But Jesus didn't clarify. He pressed further into the "eating flesh" rhetoric. He even added that people are to drink his blood (see John 6:54–56). It seemed as if Jesus was intentionally keeping this teaching complex. He allowed the people to remain perplexed, despite his loving spirit.

Sometimes, it even appeared that Jesus intentionally tried to anger his critics with complex and offensive teaching about his deity. John's Gospel contains one of these interactions between Jesus and the religious teachers who accused Jesus of having a demon (see John 8:31–59). To say that the people were offended by this teaching is an understatement. They were so put off by Jesus's words that they picked up stones to throw at him. Even though Jesus spoke truth, the people couldn't handle it at that time. Jesus knew exactly what he was doing. He chose to teach this complex truth at a unique time for his unique purposes. Jesus was the master of diagnosing the moment and adjusting his teaching methodology accordingly.

Be careful not to spend so much time trying to simplify spiritual truths for everyone to understand that you miss unique opportunities to teach in more complex ways like Jesus. Don't give in to the temptation to oversimplify your teaching. Learning to teach in a complex way at appropriate times will help make you more like Jesus in your teaching and leadership.

As I've grown, I've learned to ask myself these questions to help me determine if I should teach in a complex way: "Is there something I want to say to stretch the minds of those I am teaching? What is the spiritual maturity of those I'm teaching? Am I trying to make this truth too simple when Jesus wants it to be complex?" Pray for wisdom. Seek to be intentional as you strive to teach like Jesus.

As you read this section, you may feel frustrated. After all, the last section was about teaching simply. You might wonder, "Which is it: simple or complex?" Generally speaking, I believe we should seek to teach in the simplest way possible. However, the ultimate goal is not to be simple or complex; the goal is to be like Jesus. So, don't limit your teaching arsenal to one teaching style. That would be like a baseball player who learns how to hit only one type of pitch, a barista who can serve only one kind of coffee, or an instrumentalist who can play only one note.

Although we can't be Jesus, by God's Holy Spirit we *can* teach and lead God's people in understanding his deep truths by intentionally teaching in varied ways. Be prepared. Be prayerful. Be intentional. Learn to diagnose the situation and adapt.

Jesus Sometimes Taught in Revolutionary Ways

Sometimes the truths that Jesus taught were quite revolutionary. At times these truths seemed far-fetched, or even contrary, to what Jesus's listeners already knew. Consider Jesus's discussion about faith. Jesus said, "You don't have enough faith. . . . I tell you the truth, if you had faith even as small as a mustard seed, you could say to this mountain, 'Move from here to there,' and it would move. Nothing would be impossible" (Matthew 17:20–21). The Jewish people would have known of faith, but this was a new understanding of faith. Jesus was teaching them that a minuscule amount of faith could accomplish gigantic miracles of God.

It was also a regular occurrence for the twelve disciples to encounter radical truth from Jesus. Generally speaking, the disciples were considered uneducated men (see Acts 4:13). Yet, they developed an eagerness to learn. At times, though, this eagerness turned into an unhealthy desire to gain position with Jesus. They were so bold even to ask Jesus how they might become the greatest, and they argued about which of them was the greatest. Matthew records this moment when they asked about greatness:

> About that time the disciples came to Jesus and asked, "Who is greatest in the Kingdom of Heaven?"
> Jesus called a little child to him and put the child among them. Then he said, "I tell you the truth, unless you turn from your sins and become like little children, you will never get into the Kingdom

of Heaven. So anyone who becomes as humble as this little child is the greatest in the Kingdom of Heaven. (Matthew 18:1–4)

Jesus taught something that seemed new and different by using what was simple. He taught that greatness is found in humility. Rather than teaching his disciples to try and become special, Jesus taught them to try to be like little children. Jesus taught a similar truth later when he taught his disciples to become servants if they wanted to be the greatest in the kingdom of heaven (see Mark 9:33–37). This idea of servanthood being greater than power would contradict what the disciples experienced and observed in their culture. Neither the powerful Romans nor the influential religious leaders were known for their humility. Jesus was teaching revolutionary truth.

Multiple examples of Jesus leading by teaching groundbreaking truth fill the pages of the Gospels. For example, Jesus instructed his followers to offer abundant forgiveness. Listen to how Jesus responded to Peter when the disciple asked how often others should be forgiven. Peter asked, "Lord, how often should I forgive someone who sins against me? Seven times?" (Matthew 18:21). Jesus replied, "No, not seven times . . . but seventy times seven!" (Matthew 18:22). Additionally, Jesus taught that a person must be willing to give up all to inherit eternal life (see Luke 18:18-30). He also revealed that it's not what goes into a person that makes them unclean but instead what comes out of a person that makes them unclean (see Mark 7:5–23). Elsewhere, Jesus revealed that a poor widow who gave only two small coins to the temple offering was more generous than those rich people who gave large amounts (see Mark 12:41–44).

All these lessons from Jesus, and many others, have impacted followers of Jesus for generations. Some of these radical realities have changed the lives of individuals, families, communities, churches, and civilizations. Here's the lesson I'm learning about how to teach this way: I must teach that the ways of God are so much greater than the ways of man. Jesus-like leaders must be ready to share the truth of God with those they lead, even (or especially) when it is counter to what they already know. We can't just settle for what is easily accepted. We must strive to teach truth as Jesus taught. Revolutionary leaders share revolutionary truth, which leads to revolutionary change.

Jesus Taught with Repetition

Do you ever feel like you're saying the same thing repeatedly, and you still can't get those you are teaching to retain what you want them to retain? If so, take heart: Jesus went through that same experience. As Jesus lived out the role of a teaching leader, he frequently used repetition to teach others.

Remember when Jesus taught in the parable of the lost sheep how important one lost sinner is to God (see Luke 15:1–7)? Well, apparently Jesus thought this truth was worth sharing again. Jesus said in Luke 15:8–10:

> Or suppose a woman has ten silver coins and loses one. Won't she light a lamp and sweep the entire house and search carefully until she finds it? And when she finds it, she will call in her friends and neighbors and say, "Rejoice with me because I have found my lost coin." In the same way, there is joy in the presence of God's angels when even one sinner repents.

A few verses later, Jesus repeats this truth again when he delivers the parable of the lost son. In this parable, the father of the lost son speaks to his other son, who is jealous of the father's celebration of finding his lost son. He says, "We had to celebrate this happy day. For your brother was dead and has come back to life! He was lost, but now he is found!" (Luke 15:32). Jesus continued to repeat this idea of going after those who were lost and then celebrating once they were found. He wanted to make sure that people caught this truth. In fact, he condemned the religious leaders in his audience by portraying them as the older son who does *not* celebrate.

I can tell you from experience that people can quickly forget what you taught them. Earlier this year, I taught through a sermon series in the book of

Ephesians. I really hammered home some key themes from the book throughout the series. I knew these critical doctrines could be formative to the spiritual lives of our church members. A few days ago, while teaching a different series, I referenced some of the truths I taught in Ephesians. The blank stares I received let me know that a large portion of the congregation didn't exactly retain every word from the series in Ephesians. You see, we so easily forget what we've been taught. In fact, sometimes *I* forget what I preached the week before! Jesus recognized, and so must we, that learners need repetition.

Sometimes you may feel like a broken record. You may have to repeat your church's vision statement every week for several months before a single person can even remember part of it. You may have to retrain a staff member on how to complete a task more than once. You may reteach the same biblical truth to your core group of leaders again and again. Don't be *discouraged* because people aren't remembering. Be *encouraged* that you are teaching and leading as Jesus taught and led.

I suspect people thought Jesus, too, sounded like a broken record at times. He repeatedly taught the reality of his coming arrest, crucifixion, and resurrection. Mark 8:31 says, "Then Jesus began to tell them that the Son of Man must suffer many terrible things and be rejected by the elders, the leading priests, and the teachers of religious law. He would be killed, but three days later he would rise from the dead." Another time while gathered in Galilee, Jesus said to his followers, "The Son of Man is going to be betrayed into the hands of his enemies. He will be killed, but on the third day he will be raised from the dead" (Matthew 17:22–23). The disciples were filled with grief. Again, in Matthew 20:18–19, Jesus said, "Listen . . . we're going up to Jerusalem, where the Son of Man will be betrayed to the leading priests and the teachers of religious law. They will sentence him to die. Then they will hand him over to the Romans to be mocked, flogged with a whip, and crucified. But on the third day he will be raised from the dead." Shortly before his crucifixion, Jesus would say again, "As you know, Passover begins in two days, and the Son of Man will be handed over to be crucified" (Matthew 26:2).

Why so much repetition? Apparently, Jesus knew how fickle his disciples were—and we, too, are—and how challenging it can be for us to comprehend something. Jesus wanted his followers to grasp the important realities he was sharing with them, so he patiently repeated the same truths over and over. He led, in part, by teaching with the art of repetition.

Some teachers may seek only to check the box as they teach. They cover the content and then move on. Don't do that. People will forget what you said time and again. People will be hard-headed and hard-hearted. Don't give up. Don't lose heart. After all, you and I don't always learn the first time either. As you lead, be like Jesus. Be creative, patient, and persistent in your teaching. Teach and lead the Jesus way.

Conclusion

Teaching was integral to the leadership of Jesus. If you want to lead the Jesus way, you will strive to master the skill of teaching others. You will seek to be wise. You will look for opportunities to teach people in multiple settings and seek to use a variety of different teaching methodologies. You can do this. You can teach and lead like Jesus.

Suzanne, our small group director from the beginning of the chapter, has come a long way in her leadership. She's reminded herself that although she's been leading in the church for years, not all of her group leaders have. She has committed to passing on what leaders have spent years teaching her. Now she spends a few minutes of each small-group-leader meeting sharing tips and research for teaching effective small groups. She shares best practices for how to empower others. She prays that her group leaders may learn and develop the skills necessary to be the leaders God has called them to be. She is learning to lead like Jesus did through teaching.

This chapter pointed us to the third guidepost of leading the Jesus way: teaching people. Teaching people is one thing, but they need to move beyond just learning; people need to develop. That's the subject of chapter 4.

Key Takeaways from This Chapter
1. Leading the Jesus way means teaching with wisdom.
2. Leading the Jesus way involves teaching large groups of people.
3. Leading the Jesus way involves teaching small groups of people.
4. Leading the Jesus way means sometimes teaching simple spiritual truths.
5. Leading the Jesus way means sometimes teaching complex spiritual truths.
6. Leading the Jesus way means sometimes teaching revolutionary truth.
7. Leading the Jesus way means teaching with repetition.

Action Steps for Leaders
1. Search the Bible for wisdom and pray that God will bless you as you do.
2. Think of different contexts where you can teach those you lead.
3. Identify times when it is appropriate to teach in a simple way and when it is appropriate to teach in a complex way.
4. Challenge yourself to teach biblical truth that may be revolutionary to your hearers.
5. Identify something you are trying to teach others that would be effectively taught using repetition.

4
Developing the Next Leaders

I LEARNED SOMETHING GROWING UP. I'm not sure if somebody intentionally taught me it or if I just picked it up from a variety of places. It was this: if you want something done right, you need to do it yourself.

I've felt that way many times in my life and ministry. I've asked someone to perform a task, only to have to go behind them and do it over. I've entrusted an announcement to someone, only to hear them say it incorrectly. I've instructed someone how to follow up with a guest from church, only to have them forget. This experience is so frustrating. If I want something done right, I need to do it myself.

The problem with that mindset is that it is unbiblical and unhelpful. Leading on my own is not the Jesus way of leadership.

Leaders lead others. That is leadership in general. However, *lasting* leadership is more than *leading* others; lasting leadership *develops* others. Early in my ministry, someone taught me I would know if I was an effective leader if the ministry I led carried on after I left. I learned that effective leaders leave a lasting impact—and they do that by raising up and equipping other leaders.

This lasting impact was present in the leadership of Jesus. He equipped and developed leaders who would carry on his work long after he left the earth. Jesus did not just lead; he led by multiplying leaders. To lead like Jesus, we must also develop others. We must become leadership multipliers.

Jesus Was a Recruiter

When someone recruits me for something, it makes me feel valued. Perhaps somebody recruited you for a particular job. Maybe you were recruited to serve in the military. Maybe a lab partner chose you or the coach picked you to be a part of the basketball team when you were in school. When someone recruits you, it lets you know that they want you on their team. Well, Jesus wanted people on his team. His plan wasn't to do all the work alone. Instead, he planned and purposed to recruit others to be a part of a team who would change the world.

A great example of Jesus recruiting others is his calling of the twelve apostles:

> One day as Jesus was walking along the shore of the Sea of Galilee, he saw two brothers—Simon, also called Peter, and Andrew—throwing a net into the water, for they fished for a living. Jesus called out to them, "Come, follow me, and I will show you how to fish for people!" And they left their nets at once and followed him.
> A little farther up the shore he saw two other brothers, James and John, sitting in a boat with their father, Zebedee, repairing their nets. And he called them to come, too. They immediately followed him, leaving the boat and their father behind. (Matthew 4:18–22)

This action of Jesus was expert-level recruiting. Jesus invited Peter, Andrew, James, and John to join him for something great, and they dropped what they were doing to follow him. By the way, this moment wasn't even the first time Jesus had met these men (see John 1:40–42). He was intentional to call them to something greater from the very first moment he met them.

The calling of Matthew (also known as Levi) was another amazing recruitment (I mentioned him earlier in the book). Matthew was a tax collector, whom Jewish society did not receive well. Yet Jesus knew that God could use Matthew to be a part of his team. Luke 5:27–28 describes this moment: "Later, as Jesus left the town, he saw a tax collector named Levi sitting at his tax collector's booth. 'Follow me and be my disciple,' Jesus said to him. So Levi got up, left everything, and followed him." Matthew left everything in order to follow Jesus. Jesus chose him not just to be led but to be a leader. Jesus recruited twelve such men to follow him (you can read the full list of Jesus's disciples in Luke 6:12–16). As these twelve men followed Jesus, he multiplied his leadership and ministry through them.

Leadership development is the Jesus way. Churches are not meant to be led by lone-wolf leaders. To lead the Jesus way, we must purposefully and continually recruit others. As we learned in chapter 1, Jesus was not looking to recruit those considered the "movers and shakers" of the world. He wasn't looking for the most attractive, the most talented, or the most popular. He was looking for the willing. Jesus recruited ordinary people and even those whom others despised. Likewise, as you recruit others, look first and foremost for those willing to learn from you and follow Jesus. One of my mentors told me long ago, "Press into those who press into you." If you invite others to grow as leaders and they are willing to follow, lead them and equip them to be leaders. Be a recruiter.

Recruiting leaders is challenging. I learned long ago that one practical first step in recruiting others is to identify those who are available, willing, and teachable. They don't have to be perfect; in fact, they won't be. They will probably need lots of development. However, there may be leadership in these people waiting to blossom. The Bible paints a picture of this reality in the lives of Jesus's twelve disciples. They were rough around the edges, but Jesus developed, empowered, and equipped them to become the leaders he would use to change the world.

When I recruit, I try to spread a wide net in a variety of ways. I recruit by engaging people one-on-one, extending a general call to a specific task, and collaborating with other leaders to identify those who may have great leadership potential. I've learned from Jesus that I have to be a persistent recruiter, always watching for others I might invest in.

The leaders God wants you to develop are out there. I remember sitting on a bus in a foreign country with a young man named Tony, who was part of our group from America. We struck up a conversation, and he began to ask me about many things related to life and ministry. I could see a spark in Tony's soul toward leadership. Since that trip, I've had chances to connect with Tony again and again. Even though Tony is not part of my church family, I've been able to encourage him as he grows as a leader.

As you do ministry, pay attention to the young student who asks you extra questions at the end of a sermon or lesson. Keep your mind open to the person who frequently inquires about your social media posts. Don't dismiss the person who expresses interest in getting lunch or coffee. Don't politely ignore the church member who asks how he can best help you. Pay attention when others affirm that student whose faith seems real, that small group leader who facilitates Bible discussion well, or that quiet member who models servanthood. Seize these opportunities. Be intentional. Be a leadership recruiter. Be like Jesus.

Jesus Set Expectations

It can be frustrating when someone recruits you without giving you any instructions or expectations. We like to know what the road ahead looks like when we are following someone. Jesus didn't reveal everything that lay ahead for his followers; however, he did tell them expectations of what it looked like to follow him. Consider Jesus's call to count the cost. In Luke 14:28–33, Jesus said,

> But don't begin until you count the cost. For who would begin construction of a building without first calculating the cost to see if there is enough money to finish it? Otherwise, you might complete only the foundation before running out of money, and then everyone would laugh at you. They would say, "There's the person who started that building and couldn't afford to finish it!"
>
> Or what king would go to war against another king without first sitting down with his counselors to discuss whether his army of 10,000 could defeat the 20,000 soldiers marching against him?

And if he can't, he will send a delegation to discuss terms of peace while the enemy is still far away. So you cannot become my disciple without giving up everything you own.

Sometimes we might even think that Jesus was a little too blunt with his expectations. In Luke 9:57–62 we learn of one such encounter:

As they were walking along, someone said to Jesus, "I will follow you wherever you go." But Jesus replied, "Foxes have dens to live in, and birds have nests, but the Son of Man has no place even to lay his head." He said to another person, "Come, follow me." The man agreed, but he said, "Lord, first let me return home and bury my father." But Jesus told him, "Let the spiritually dead bury their own dead! Your duty is to go and preach about the Kingdom of God." Another said, "Yes, Lord, I will follow you, but first let me say good-bye to my family." But Jesus told him, "Anyone who puts a hand to the plow and then looks back is not fit for the Kingdom of God."

If we're honest, we might say Jesus's responses sounded insensitive. However, it's actually the opposite. Jesus wanted people to realize what it meant to truly follow him. He wanted them to understand the expectations and urgency of following him. Jesus was more direct when he said in Matthew 16:24, "If anyone wants to follow after me, let him deny himself, take up his cross, and follow me." Taking up your cross meant you must be willing to walk to your execution. Jesus didn't deliver a pep talk. Rather, he was vivid and honest about the challenges that awaited those who followed him.

Sometimes Jesus even warned about how things might turn out for those who followed him. He said in Matthew 10:16, "Look, I'm sending you out like sheep among wolves." That's not how most textbooks would teach you to recruit followers. And yet millions of people have chosen to follow Jesus. Why? Because there is no one greater to follow, no one greater to serve, and no greater mission to achieve.

My childhood youth pastor, Keith Tarkington, had a tremendous influence on my life (shout out to all the youth pastors out there! Keep up the good work!). He continues to impact me today, both in the lasting impression he left all those years ago and in the occasional correspondence that we have. I remember a story he told of giving up ministry for a season. Instead of doing church work, he decided to work for a delivery service because ministry had worn away at him. While working that delivery route, he often had to drive by his former place of ministry. He was reminded of his call to ministry each time he drove by. He couldn't stay away long. He knew God had called him to serve in ministry, so he decided to return to vocational ministry. That story reminds me that leading the Jesus way is not easy, but it is good. We must help others learn this reality, as Keith did for me.

As you develop Christlike leaders, let them know what lies ahead. Let them know about the sleepless nights. Give them a glimpse of the murmuring and complaining that will come. Tell them of the hurt of being betrayed by someone you poured your heart and soul into. Then, tell them of the beauty of following Jesus. Tell them Jesus guaranteed he would be with them always (see Matthew 28:20). Following Jesus is not just full of sacrifice; it is also full of blessing.

Jesus Was a Motivator

Jesus was straightforward and candid when giving his expectations for his followers. However, it wasn't all difficult news when it came to following Jesus. Jesus was also a master of motivation. Despite the cost of following Jesus, many still chose to do so. These followers were motivated by the rewards of following Jesus (including simply having a relationship with Jesus himself) and the importance of the mission. To lead the Jesus way, you must also motivate those you are developing.

Jesus Motivated by Pointing out That God Rewards Faithfulness

Jesus made it clear that God would reward his followers for their faithfulness. After the sad moment when a rich man refused to give up his possessions to follow Jesus (see Matthew 19:16–22), the disciples of Jesus inquired as to whether they would be rewarded for their faithfulness to him.

> Then Peter said to him, "We've given up everything to follow you. What will we get?"
>
> Jesus replied, "I assure you that when the world is made new and the Son of Man sits upon his glorious throne, you who have been my followers will also sit on twelve thrones, judging the twelve tribes of Israel. And everyone who has given up houses or brothers or sisters or father or mother or children or property, for my sake, will receive a hundred times as much in return and will inherit eternal life." (Matthew 19:27–29)

Jesus assured his followers that what they were doing was not temporary. Instead, the work of the disciples would have eternal ramifications. His words gave them the spiritual rigor they needed to carry on the mission, particularly once he had left the earth. Jesus was a motivator.

So also we must motivate those we lead to grasp the magnitude of their ministry. We must help them realize that what they do has eternal outcomes. God sees our faithfulness, and no one rewards their children better than our heavenly Father (see Matthew 7:7–11).

Sometimes I get so caught up in planning the next meeting, answering other leaders' questions, and ensuring our church has excellence in ministry that I forget how important it is to point others to the heavenly rewards of serving Jesus. Those we lead must understand that doing the mission of God is not the same as other jobs. This work can change eternity. Leaders like Jesus must capitalize on this reality to set expectations and increase motivation among those they lead. Don't miss this opportunity. Motivate others as Jesus motivated others.

It should motivate us to know that God sees and remembers all our work. We must help those we lead realize our heavenly Father sees when we are faithful, both in the big and the little things. God is pleased when we visit those who need love. God will reward the monotonous work of setting up chairs over countless weeks. God sees every nursery volunteer who changes diapers and shows love to crying babies. God values every coin given to send the gospel to the far-reaching parts of the world. As Jesus did, we must ignite those we lead by reminding them of the promise of God's life-sustaining joy and eternal rewards for those who are faithful to him.

Jesus Motivated by Pointing out That God Empowers

Another way that Jesus motivated his followers was by proclaiming the power behind their ministry. The followers of Jesus heard him teach eternal truths, saw him work miracles, and watched him lead with conviction and integrity. Yet Jesus said in John 14:12–14, "I tell you the truth, anyone who believes in me will do the same works I have done, and even greater works, because I am going to be with the Father. You can ask for anything in my name, and I will do it, so that the Son can bring glory to the Father. Yes, ask me for anything in my name, and I will do it!" Can you imagine how the disciples felt when Jesus said that they would not only do the same works that he did but even greater works? They must have been thinking, "Are you sure?" However, they did not yet realize that the power of the Holy Spirit would come upon them when Jesus left the earth, and everything would change forever.

As my ministry developed, I realized something beautiful. I realized that I could motivate those I lead with the same foundational power that Jesus used to motivate his followers: the power of God's Holy Spirit. We can motivate those we lead by pointing out that, by God's power, they can do even greater works than Jesus did while he was on the earth. As you develop leaders, you must motivate them by reminding them of the hope, confidence, and power that come from an awareness of God's divine power that resides within them.

The Holy Spirit can give us and those we lead compassion for people we may not care about as we should. God's Spirit can enlighten us with the knowledge, words, and wisdom to teach others. God can give courage and boldness to those who may naturally be timid so they can minister in dangerous and undesirable places. The Holy Spirit can even bring reconciliation and restoration to those who have fallen in some way. God is an empowering God!

Jesus Motivated by Pointing out That God Shows Grace

I've come to realize that sometimes the best way I can motivate those I lead is by showing them a vision of grace and restoration. When someone drops the ball on an assignment, I try to remember that I've dropped the ball many times in my ministry. When someone misses an appointment with me, I double-check that I had the correct time and gently ask if they need help with effective ways to schedule meetings. When someone fumbles a teaching opportunity, I point out what they did well, give suggestions for improvement, and then look for the next time we can schedule them to teach again. Grace and restoration: that's the Jesus way to lead.

One of the most beautiful examples of grace-filled motivation in the ministry of Jesus was an encounter with Peter and the resurrected Jesus (see John 21:15–17). I mentioned this story already when I spoke of how Jesus taught Peter one-on-one. To understand the significance of this conversation between Peter and Jesus, we must remember that Peter had denied Jesus three times before Jesus was crucified (see Luke 22:54–62). Some may feel that Jesus would have been justified in giving up on Peter and never using him for ministry again, yet that wasn't how Jesus operated. Instead, Jesus motivated Peter by having a conversation with him and encouraging him to lead his people (feed his sheep). Although it was probably a hard conversation for Peter (because Jesus asked him the same question three times), it was nevertheless a pivotal moment for Peter. In fact, he would later become a foundational leader in the early church. Through grace and restoration, Jesus motivated and elevated Peter to powerful ministry.

Peter was imperfect, and we and those we lead are imperfect also. Indeed, some of the leaders we are trying to develop will surely let us down from time to time, and they may even betray us. However, filled with the love of Jesus, we must be prepared to help those who fall get back up and be used for God's purposes once again. We must motivate them to be filled with power and restoration as Jesus motivated Peter. Motivating those we develop not only sustains them for ministry, but it also continues the mission God began and is still carrying out through his church.

So, encourage those who mess up by reminding them of Peter, David, Moses, and many others whom God used despite their failures. Tell them examples from your own life of how God used you despite your imperfections and failures. Then, point them to the love of Jesus. Take them back to the grace of God. Show them Scripture that highlights God's power and our need to rely on him. Motivate them to become leaders who rely on God's deep grace and power.

Jesus Was a Deployer

Sometimes people learn to do something simply by giving it a try. Those we lead don't need to have everything figured out before they serve. Leaders need to be launched into ministry, even if they are still not fully equipped. Jesus practiced this principle as a leader. He didn't wait until his followers were top performers. Rather, he *developed* others by *deploying* them into ministry.

Early in their ministry, Jesus sent his disciples in pairs to accomplish God's mission on earth. Mark describes this moment in Mark 6:7–13:

And he called his twelve disciples together and began sending them out two by two, giving them authority to cast out evil spirits. He told them to take nothing for their journey except a walking stick— no food, no traveler's bag, no money. He allowed them to wear sandals but not to take a change of clothes. "Wherever you go," he said, "stay in the same house until you leave town. But if any place refuses to welcome you or listen to you, shake its dust from your feet as you leave to show that you have abandoned those people to their fate." So the disciples went out, telling everyone they met to repent of their sins and turn to God. And they cast out many demons and healed many sick people, anointing them with olive oil.

Consider how you can nudge others toward ministry. Maybe you can take a young leader along with you while you go on a ministry visit. Perhaps you can ask an aspiring Bible teacher to introduce the small group lesson you are teaching. You can give that growing Christian an opportunity to coordinate the greeting ministry for your next special event. Don't wait until those you are developing are perfect, or you'll be waiting a long time. Put developing leaders in places of ministry now.

When we deploy others, we often do so knowing they are inexperienced. Some may think it wise to go easy on "new recruits" when we send them out. Not Jesus. Jesus said to pack light, expect opposition, and get to work. As if they were a group of rookie athletes on the field, Jesus set loose the disciples and gave them clear expectations of what God could do through them. Jesus deployed them despite their inexperience.

Jesus also helped realign the expectations and perspectives of the disciples as he launched them into ministry. He said in Matthew 10:26–28,

But don't be afraid of those who threaten you. For the time is coming when everything that is covered will be revealed, and all that is secret will be made known to all. What I tell you now in the darkness, shout abroad when daybreak comes. What I whisper in your ear, shout from the housetops for all to hear! Don't be afraid of those who want to kill your body; they cannot touch your soul. Fear only God, who can destroy both soul and body in hell.

Jesus did not promise that everything would be easy. They weren't guaranteed worldly success. However, Jesus sent them out with power. Jesus wanted them to know God was sending them out for his mission. As

I develop other leaders, I must intentionally help realign their focus and send them out to minister for God's purposes. I must help them pay more attention to the things of God and less attention to the things of this world. Their focus and their mission must be God-centered and God-glorifying.

In my early days of ministry, some leaders gave me several ministry opportunities that were not easy. I was thoroughly inexperienced. In fact, sometimes I wondered if those overseeing my ministry training knew what they were doing. Now I understand that they knew exactly what they were doing.

One particularly challenging assignment was leading a campus ministry that met at a local public middle school in the early morning. All middle school ministries are challenging, but this one was an above-average challenge (by the way, if you can do middle school ministry, you can do any type of ministry; it's the toughest of the tough!). After just a little bit of training, I was all alone with about fifty to seventy-five kids between the ages of eleven and fourteen. Many of them were there just for the free donuts. I was barely out of high school myself, but I was expected to lead them and teach them the Bible. It wasn't an easy task, but it was God's task and God's calling for me at that time. I served at that school for several years. God was with me, and by his grace he used that opportunity for his purposes. The development that took place in my life during these years was astronomical. I wouldn't change that experience for the world.

Those we lead may feel inexperienced and unprepared. We must remind them that God is with them, and he is with them powerfully. We must tell them of how God was with Joshua, Esther, and the early church. We must tell them how God used us in our early days of ministry. We must assure them that we still cannot do anything without the power of Jesus in our lives (see John 15:5), but with him we can do all things. Lead those you are developing to put their focus on and faith in God, his ways, and his power.

When it comes to sending others into ministry, there's no more important passage than Matthew 28:18–20. This passage has come to be known as the "Great Commission," and, indeed, it is great. Matthew records these famous words:

Jesus came and told his disciples, "I have been given all authority in heaven and on earth. Therefore, go and make disciples of all the nations, baptizing them in the name of the Father and the Son and the Holy Spirit. Teach these new disciples to obey all the commands I have given you. And be sure of this: I am with you always, even to the end of the age."

The scope of this commission is great, both in the breadth of work and in the responsibility on whom it falls. With the Great Commission, Jesus launched all of his followers into ministry. All of us must "go" and minister in the name of the Father, Son, and Holy Spirit. As leaders who lead the Jesus way, we must carry on the work of Jesus in commissioning others to minister in the name of Jesus. We must develop disciples who develop disciples to minister for the glory of God.

Take some time and think about how this might play out in your ministry. For example, after someone you are developing teaches a lesson to youth or children, give him pointers on how to better connect with the learners. Remind those who lead the welcome team to smile when they greet guests. Lovingly point out to the coordinator of the community ministry event how she can do a better job completing administrative tasks ahead of time. Don't expect perfection from those you lead; however, don't settle for lack of development either. God's design and desire for us are that we would continually develop.

Developing others will get messy along the way. The disciples frequently messed up. They were unable to cast out demons at times (see Matthew 17:19), wanted to call down fire on those to whom Jesus was ministering (see Luke 9:51–56), and one cut off the ear of somebody who stood against Jesus (see John 19:10). That's not even the entire list of their mistakes. Here's the point: eventually, you must launch those you are developing. You can't wait until everything lines up perfectly. If you try, you will never develop leaders, because none of us is perfect. Trust me: God can work through imperfect leaders and imperfect followers. Not only do we see that in the Bible, but seasoned leaders can verify that reality in their own lives and ministries. Lead like Jesus: develop leaders and launch them into ministry.

I've had some great developers in my life. Two particular men who have multiplied leadership in my own life are Kevin Ezell and Jimmy Scroggins— both of whom I've mentioned already in this book. In the early 2000s, these two men worked in tandem to raise dozens of ministry leaders who spread out all over the world to impact the kingdom of God. They developed others who would serve as pastors, leaders, businesspeople, godly parents, missionaries, seminary professors, and more. Kevin Ezell and Jimmy Scroggins are not only masters of leadership development, they are leaders who lead the Jesus way.

My first encounter with these two men came when I was a student at Southern Seminary in Louisville, Kentucky. During my first week in Louisville, I visited Highview Baptist Church. Highview impacted me so much that I never visited another church during the entire five and a half years I lived in Louisville. Kevin Ezell was the pastor of Highview at the time, and Jimmy Scroggins was the youth pastor.

The secret sauce behind Kevin's and Jimmy's leadership development was a robust internship program. From a very early age (eighteen for me), young leaders were allowed to learn and lead in local church settings. These learning experiences involved leading small groups, working with adult volunteers, planning special events, going on mission trips, working with local schools, teaching the Bible, and attending weekly intern staff meetings. It's no understatement to say that this experience changed my life. There's no way to measure how much impact Kevin and Jimmy had on me. To this day, they are still encouraging and teaching me. Kevin and Jimmy both left Highview for other leadership roles, but their legacy continues.

Conclusion

"If you want something done correctly, do it yourself."

That was the lie I believed in my early years of ministry. I thought that I could do much more on my own than I truly could. I viewed others in ministry as a roadblock or even competition. Jesus has changed me.

Now I see others as prospective teammates or partners in ministry. I see the potential within others, just waiting to blossom through God's anointing. Now I say to myself, "Wow, imagine what kind of leader God could turn that person into!" Jesus was a developer, and by God's grace he can use us to develop others as well.

Set your mind on being a developer. Recognize the God-given opportunities to be one who multiplies the mission of Jesus for generations to come. Leadership development is a beautiful chain of blessings. Godly leadership can impact multiple churches, change multiple cultures, and lead to the rescue of multiple lives. Be a leader who leads the Jesus way. Be a leadership developer.

The Jesus-inspired leadership guidepost of this chapter has been "developing people." But what do we do when we face opposition? Keep reading and find out.

Key Takeaways from This Chapter
1. Leading the Jesus way means being a recruiter.
2. Leading the Jesus way means setting expectations.
3. Leading the Jesus way means motivating those you develop.
4. Leading the Jesus way means deploying others into ministry.

Action Steps for Leaders
1. Identify potential leaders you can recruit.
2. Establish clear expectations for the top volunteer leaders in your church.
3. Ask a leader you trust from another church how they best motivate those they lead.
4. Set a goal to deploy one new person into a leadership position in the next thirty days.

5
Leading Despite Opposition

IT'S A BLESSING TO LEAD THE JESUS WAY. Being used by God to lead his people is one of the amazing gifts God bestows upon church leaders. I count my role as a church leader as one of the greatest joys of my life, outside of being a follower of Jesus, a husband, and a father. Yet, leading the Jesus way is not without difficulty. I will talk in this chapter about some of the opposition you may encounter as you lead, but I do so with the hope that you will not be discouraged. Read this carefully: if God is calling you to lead, he will be faithful to sustain you, even in the face of opposition. Lead on.

I quickly learned of the reality of opposition when I began my first pastorate. When I came, the church was in quite a mess. They had been through a distressing experience that led to multiple divisions in the church. There was a lot of hurt, and it multiplied. As the old saying goes, "Hurting people hurt people."

Indeed, I experienced some hurtful situations when I first came. The memory of a couple who sat in my office in my early days as the pastor is still fresh. This couple demanded I make a decision I knew would be not only foolish but also evil. When I told them I could make no such decision, they said they would leave the church if I didn't do things their way. So they left the church and later lied to others about our conversation. It was a painful moment. I had barely started as the leader, and my momentum seemed to be coming to a screeching halt. Opposition came early.

If you will lead the Jesus way, accept that you will lead in the face of opposition. Jesus said of his own ministry in Luke 12:51, "Do you think I have come to bring peace to the earth? No, I have come to divide people against each other!" There is much to say about what Jesus meant in Luke 12, but it means no less than this: a ministry like the ministry of Jesus will not always be peaceful. Ultimately, the ministry of Jesus would lead to such resistance that he would be betrayed, arrested, beaten, and crucified. Jesus-like leadership breeds opposition. Be prepared, and be encouraged that you are leading like Jesus.

Jesus Faced Opposition from Outsiders

Several years ago I witnessed a pastor friend face outside opposition. He had been at his church for several years and was trying to make changes to their governing documents. Most of his church family seemed to agree with the proposed changes. Then came the primary voice of opposition. A leader in the network this pastor was part of came to speak against the direction of the church leaders. What particularly irked me was that this opposer didn't even attend that church. This experience stirred some anger in me that still burns today. The pastor was a friend of mine, and I couldn't believe someone would be so bold to interfere in the life of a local church in such a manner.

The story of my pastor friend ended well. Some godly church members stood up to the outside bully, and he didn't get his way. Also, the pastor had enough credibility, grace, and wisdom to navigate the situation. I learned from watching my friend face that situation, though, that Christlike leaders will sometimes face opposition from outsiders.

Of course, many outsiders also opposed the work of Jesus. The Pharisees were perhaps the most famous of those who opposed the work of Jesus. These guys were constantly questioning the work of Jesus and his disciples. They even said that Jesus's father was the devil (see John 8:44). You might say they were professional opposers. It's not surprising, then, that Jesus didn't always have pleasant things to say about them, either. In fact, Jesus said in Matthew 12:34, "You brood of snakes! How could evil men like you speak what is good and right?"

The Pharisees didn't slow down Jesus's ministry, despite their constant opposition to him. On the contrary, it seemed that Jesus had no concern about upsetting the religious leaders of his day. For example, consider when he cleared the temple.

> When they arrived back in Jerusalem, Jesus entered the Temple and began to drive out the people buying and selling animals for sacrifices. He knocked over the tables of the money changers and the chairs of those selling doves, and he stopped everyone from using the Temple as a marketplace. He said to them, "The Scriptures declare, 'My Temple will be called a house of prayer for all nations,' but you have turned it into a den of thieves." (Mark 11:15–17)

We don't have to wonder how the Jewish leaders reacted: "When the leading priests and teachers of religious law heard what Jesus had done, they began planning how to kill him" (Mark 11:18). That's intense opposition! Jesus pressed on.

Jesus also encountered a general disregard toward his effort to help people. Consider one time when the Pharisees sought to trap Jesus while he healed a man. Matthew 12:9–14 says,

> Then Jesus went over to their synagogue, where he noticed a man with a deformed hand. The Pharisees asked Jesus, "Does the law permit a person to work by healing on the Sabbath?" (They were hoping he would say yes, so they could bring charges against him.)
> And he answered, "If you had a sheep that fell into a well on the Sabbath, wouldn't you work to pull it out? Of course you would. And how much more valuable is a person than a sheep! Yes, the law permits a person to do good on the Sabbath."
> Then he said to the man, "Hold out your hand." So the man held out his hand, and it was restored, just like the other one! Then the Pharisees called a meeting to plot how to kill Jesus.

These men were so opposed to the work of Jesus that they were trying to stop him from doing the good of healing a man. After they failed to trap him, they were so angry that they devised a plan to kill him. The next time you have a group who strongly opposes your ministry, remember that you are in good company with Jesus.

Jesus even faced rejection from those who barely knew him. While traveling to Jerusalem, Jesus sent word to a Samaritan village that he would pass through. Many towns would have been glad to have Jesus travel their way. However, these Samaritan townspeople were different. Luke 9:53–55 says, "But the people of the village did not welcome Jesus because he was on his way to Jerusalem. When James and John saw this, they said to Jesus, 'Lord, should we call down fire from heaven to burn them up?' But Jesus turned and rebuked them." James and John were so offended on behalf of Jesus that they wanted to see these Samaritans destroyed. Jesus continued his ministry.

As you lead, outside opposition is sure to come your way. Not everyone will understand your motivations or your ministry. While you should plan that external opposition may come, you should also plan to persevere through it. Jesus pressed on, and so can you. Be like Jesus as you lead.

Jesus Faced Opposition from His Own

It's one thing for outsiders, like the Samaritans, to reject Jesus and his ministry, but it must have been particularly hurtful when Jesus's own people rejected him. John says in John 12:37, "But despite all the miraculous signs Jesus had done, most of the people still did not believe in him." Let that sink in: *despite* his miracles, people didn't believe. The people should have praised, thanked, and exalted Jesus for his ministry. Instead of awe and wonder, though, they displayed disbelief. We must remember that reality as we seek to lead the Jesus way. Even if it were possible for us to lead as powerfully and effectively as Jesus led, we would still face rejection.

Imagine that you were in the shoes of Jesus for a moment (I know that's hard to do). Imagine that you had been preparing thirty years for your ministry. Then, you finally begin, only to encounter opposition from those who know you best. Matthew tells us that Jesus lived this reality when those in his hometown of Nazareth rejected him. Matthew 13:54–57 says,

> He returned to Nazareth, his hometown. When he taught there in the synagogue, everyone was amazed and said, "Where does he get this wisdom and the power to do miracles?" Then they scoffed, "He's just the carpenter's son, and we know Mary, his mother, and his brothers—James, Joseph, Simon, and Judas. All his sisters live right here among us. Where did he learn all these things?" And they were deeply offended and refused to believe in him. Then Jesus told them, "A prophet is honored everywhere except in his own hometown and among his own family."

Jesus was certainly not surprised by this rejection. Likewise, we should not be surprised when we face rejection, even from those who know us.

Well, what about Jesus's family? Surely his family would never reject him. In fact, they would. We learn in John 7:3–5 that "Jesus' brothers said to him, 'Leave here and go to Judea, where your followers can see your miracles! You can't become famous if you hide like this! If you can do such wonderful things, show yourself to the world!' For even his brothers didn't believe in him." During his earthly ministry, his brothers not only rejected his ministry, but they also mocked him.

Though I've not experienced what Jesus went through, I have felt rejection from those within my circle of influence. For example, a former church member recently told others she didn't want to come to the church facility if I was there. Even though I had invested in her, shown love to her family, and even helped her in difficult times, she still openly opposed me. I couldn't think of anything I had done to warrant such an attitude. This experience was challenging, although it was not shocking. Opposition is a part of leadership—even opposition from those you know and love.

Sometimes we even experience opposition from those closest to our ministry. Earlier in my ministry career, one of my own volunteer team members spoke badly about me and my decision making. This person even accused me of putting those under my care in a harmful situation (which was not true). Obviously, this was a difficult situation for me. I had hoped this person would have been a help in what God was doing in my ministry, not a hindrance. It hurt to be opposed by one of my own.

Jesus also experienced opposition from those who were closest to his ministry. He even anticipated that this would happen. Jesus predicted that Peter, one of his most passionate followers, would outright deny Jesus. In fact, Jesus predicted that all the apostles would reject him, yet Peter spoke up. Mark 14:29–30 says, "Peter said to him, 'Even if everyone else deserts you, I never will.' Jesus replied, 'I tell you the truth, Peter—this very night, before the rooster crows twice, you will deny three times that you even know me.'" Jesus was correct. Peter would deny him. Even though Jesus knew this moment was coming, I can't imagine how painful it must have been for him when it happened.

You may recall that Jesus was betrayed by and arrested because of one of his closest followers. Luke 22:47–48 describes the moment that Judas betrayed Jesus: "But even as Jesus said this, a crowd approached, led by Judas, one of the twelve disciples. Judas walked over to Jesus to greet him with a kiss. But Jesus said, 'Judas, would you betray the Son of Man with a kiss?'" Jesus knew what was going to happen. He knew he would be betrayed, arrested, and crucified, yet he ministered anyway. You will likely not suffer the same betrayal and death that Jesus suffered; however, you will likely face rejection. Anticipate it, and when you experience it, remember that your Lord also faced rejection.

Sometimes I feel discouraged because a church member I invested much in leaves my church. Perhaps someone I prayed with after losing a loved one complained that I didn't spend enough time ministering to him or her. Or a young intern who I have poured countless hours into suddenly leaves for a more glamorous ministry opportunity.

Have you ever been there? Have you ever felt discouraged when someone rejected you or your ministry? Well, Jesus experienced this as well. Yet he continued his ministry, and it changed the world forever. Don't lose heart. If you give up on leadership, you'll miss all that God wants to do through your ministry. You'll miss the beauty of seeing a dying church return to life; you'll never see that young woman who was lost in addiction become a godly wife and mother; you'll not have the opportunity to pray for that young man who surrenders his life to go reach unreached people on the mission field. Opposition is temporary, but kingdom ministry has eternal rewards. Lead on.

Jesus Faced Opposition from Evil Spiritual Forces

As if human rejection were not enough, Jesus also encountered spiritual opposition from evil forces. God prophesied that Satan would oppose Jesus long before Jesus even came to the earth as a baby. Immediately following the entrance of sin into the world, God said to the serpent (Satan): "And I will cause hostility between you and the woman, and between your offspring and her offspring. He will strike your head, and you will strike his heel" (Genesis 3:15). Indeed, the forces of Satan constantly struck at the heel of Jesus for his entire ministry.

The powers of evil were set against Jesus from the very beginning of his time on the earth. The king of the land wanted to kill Jesus when he was just a small child. Matthew 2:13 says, "an angel of the Lord appeared to Joseph in a dream. 'Get up! Flee to Egypt with the child and his mother,' the angel said. 'Stay there until I tell you to return, because Herod is going to search for the child to kill him.'" Likewise, just before the launch of his ministry, Jesus faced direct temptation from the devil (see Matthew 4:1–11). The enemy tempted him multiple times, and each time Jesus rejected Satan's temptation with the Word of God.

Satan is so deceptive and cunning that he even worked directly through some of Jesus's apostles. Jesus even referred to Peter as "Satan" at one point because he was standing in the way of the work of Jesus (more on this later). However, at other times, Satan worked more directly through the disciples. Luke tells us in Luke 22:3, "Then Satan entered into Judas Iscariot, who was one of the twelve disciples." Judas went on to betray Jesus to the Jewish authorities. Make no mistake; Judas was responsible for his actions. At the same time, demonic forces were at work in him.

After Jesus left the earth, his apostles not only continued Jesus's mission, but they also continued to experience demonic opposition. They were jailed, persecuted, killed, and rejected—and they were victorious. The church thrived and multiplied under the apostles' ministry. The continued faithfulness of the apostles led to the establishment of pastors, deacons, and churches throughout the ancient world. The same mission of Jesus remains today!

If we are doing the work of Jesus, the forces of evil will not sit by idly. Satan will seek to stand against us, often through temptation and opposition. Don't be defeated; instead, be ready. Dive into Ephesians 6:10–17 and discover the armor of God that is available for the follower of Jesus. Heed the words of Paul in verse 11: "Put on all of God's armor so that you will be able to stand firm against all strategies of the devil."

When we face opposition from Satan and his evil forces, we encounter the same opposition Jesus faced. And, through the Holy Spirit, we can have the same victory Jesus had. Remember Jesus's words: "I will build my church, and all the powers of hell will not conquer it" (Matthew 16:18). Don't give up, and don't give in. Stay faithful as you lead the Jesus way.

Frustrations Are Not Necessarily Opposition

At times you may find yourself diligently working to lead your people toward the vision God has laid on your heart, only to have those you serve alongside derail the momentum. I remember trying to build positivity and unity in my first years as pastor of our church. A person who brought a trivial or selfish complaint could instantly crush all that positive energy. In one church I served, church members were offering outdated ideas for outreach and trying to preserve certain aspects of worship simply because it was "the way we've always done it." The optimism I had for moving toward a healthy biblical church was slowly being drained from me. These kinds of situations can be downright frustrating, but they may not necessarily be opposition.

Sometimes those who seem to be opposition may instead be experiencing difficult times in their lives. Perhaps they are spiritually malnourished due to years of lacking discipleship or godly leadership. A previous leader may have hurt those under your influence, making them reluctant to trust a new leader fully. Don't lose heart. Although frustrating, these people may not intentionally oppose you or your leadership.

Some of what Jesus experienced in his leadership would surely be frustrating to most leaders. Although he led as a servant, willingly putting the needs of others ahead of his own, his followers were trying to outdo one another in greatness. In Mark 10 we learn that James and John were trying to convince Jesus to consider them for something significant. They wanted to be the greatest in the kingdom of heaven. They were literally asking to have special seats next to Jesus. As you can imagine, once the other disciples heard this, they were not happy. Mark 10:41 says, "When the ten other disciples heard what James and John had asked, they were indignant." Why were they indignant? Because *they* each wanted to be the most significant follower of Jesus. James and John were displaying desires that went against the ways of Jesus, although they were not intentionally opposing Jesus. Instead of replicating the servant-oriented leadership of Jesus, they were fighting for the selfish-oriented power of the world.

Jesus was so put off by Peter's behavior on one occasion that he said Peter was acting like the devil. Matthew describes this moment to us in Matthew 16:21–23.

> From then on Jesus began to tell his disciples plainly that it was necessary for him to go to Jerusalem, and that he would suffer many terrible things at the hands of the elders, the leading priests, and the teachers of religious law. He would be killed, but on the third day he would be raised from the dead.
>
> But Peter took him aside and began to reprimand him for saying such things. "Heaven forbid, Lord," he said. "This will never happen to you!"

Jesus turned to Peter and said, "Get away from me, Satan! You are a dangerous trap to me. You are seeing things merely from a human point of view, not from God's."

The primary mission of Jesus was to give his life as a payment for sins. Yet, Peter was trying to prevent Jesus from carrying out his mission. Here's the thing: Peter may have had good intentions in trying to prevent Jesus from being killed. He was not purposefully trying to oppose Jesus, but Peter's actions contradicted Jesus's mission.

Perhaps you remember the famous moment when Peter cut off the ear of the high priest's servant (see John 18:10–11). This ear-slashing took place when the Jewish leaders came to arrest Jesus. Jesus stopped everything and healed the servant's ear (see Luke 22:51). I imagine Jesus probably wanted to say, "Peter, would you just stop and let me do what I came to do!"

I can identify with the frustration of Jesus (in a smaller way). In one of my previous roles, I was a missions pastor. I often led teams from our church into different cultures seeking to display the love of God and share the gospel of Jesus Christ. Many times I felt like I spent a lot of my energy making sure that someone from our team didn't somehow hinder our ministry. I was hopeful that someone from our team didn't complain about the local food. I was keenly aware that a team member might refuse to take their shoes off in a sacred place. It was even possible for someone to cause offense to a town leader that a local Christian leader had been trying to minister to for years. Certain actions by team members could seem to oppose the work we came to do, albeit unintentionally.

As church leaders, we may experience times when those we lead try to do what they think is correct, buy they end up creating more headaches and challenges for us to sort out. There will be obstacles along the path, sometimes from our own followers. Dealing well with these frustrations is part of what it means to lead the Jesus way.

You, too, may face these challenges. Perhaps you're spending much of your time and energy "healing ears" (fixing problems) when those you lead are "swinging swords" (making problems). But again, this is leading the Jesus way. Be patient. These frustrations may eventually lead to celebrations. Continue to minister; continue to lead. The ministry at hand is important. Those you lead are important. Press on!

Jesus Pressed on Despite Opposition

I'm not sure I'm comfortable expressing all that might go through my mind if I faced the full force of rejection Jesus faced. I may also want to call down fire from heaven from time to time (as James and John suggested). That's not leading the Jesus way. Jesus was focused on the mission, not on himself. Jesus pressed on, and so should we.

Continue to lead, even when others oppose or reject you. Ask yourself if the person who caused you such angst really has that much influence in your life and ministry. Keep a file of all the times people encouraged you or spoke well of your leadership, and use those reminders to pick yourself up when someone else knocks you down. Rally like-minded people around you to help keep you on the path God has led you to follow. Remind yourself that Jesus is ultimately the one you serve.

As we lead amid opposition, it's fruitful to remind ourselves that we were once in opposition to God. Before Jesus rescued us from sin, we were ourselves enemies of the cross. Indeed, Paul explained in Romans 5:8–11,

> But God showed his great love for us by sending Christ to die for us while we were still sinners. And since we have been made right in God's sight by the blood of Christ, he will certainly save us from God's condemnation. For since our friendship with God was restored by the death of his Son while we were still his enemies, we will certainly be saved through the life of his Son. So now we can rejoice in our wonderful new relationship with God because our Lord Jesus Christ has made us friends of God.

So, when others are against you, remember that you were once against God. Thank God for his grace in your life. Learn how to show grace to others. God's grace saved you, and God's grace will sustain you.

Ministry is hard. Leadership is hard. Still, God is always good. During difficulty, we need to remember God's message to the apostle Paul as he faced great anguish: "My grace is all you need. My power works best in weakness" (2 Corinthians 12:9). God's grace is also sufficient for you. His power works best in your weakness, including when opposition and frustration drain you as a leader.

Indeed, Hebrews 10:39 (ESV) says, "But we are not of those who shrink back and are destroyed, but of those who have faith and preserve their souls." To lead the Jesus way means we stand tall with God's strength and continue moving forward, even when times get tough. God would not call you to a mission and ministry that he did not intend for you to complete. So, lead the Jesus way. Press on and lead in the face of opposition.

Conclusion

The story I told at the beginning of the chapter about the couple who left our church may still be in my mind, but it doesn't sting like it once did. I've learned from the life and ministry of Jesus that if you're doing the work of God, you should expect opposition. Sometimes I still get blindsided by an act of evil, selfishness, or foolishness. That's okay. God has not called me to lead only in the easy times. He's called me to lead in the tough times as well. He's called me to lead the Jesus way.

Remember, each chapter of this book will show us a guidepost that directs us down the path of Jesus-like leadership. At this point, we've addressed the guideposts of prioritizing people, seeing and meeting needs, teaching people, developing people, and leading despite opposition. Finally, let's find out how we can prioritize what's important. That's the topic of our final chapter.

Key Takeaways from this Chapter

1. Jesus led, even when outsiders opposed him.
2. Jesus led, even when his own opposed him.
3. Jesus led, even when evil forces opposed him.
4. Jesus led, even when he experienced frustration from others.

Action Steps for Leaders:

1. Identify some rejection you've faced in your ministry. How did that affect you?
2. Consider a Christlike way you can respond when those you lead interfere with your ministry.
3. Commit to calling a trusted friend the next time you face outside opposition.
4. Journal about what the Bible says concerning the victory of the Christian in the presence of evil forces.

6
Prioritizing What's Most Important

CHARLES HAS BEEN A YOUTH PASTOR at Hillsboro AME Church for six months. He loves his job. Ever since he came to Christ, he felt a call to gospel ministry. But lately, ministry is getting difficult for him. He seems to be fighting just to keep his head above water.

Charles is a hard worker, an eager learner, and a sharp leader. He's precisely the kind of young minister Hillsboro AME Church is glad to have. The problem is, because he's such an exceptional young minister, Charles has begun to have more ministry than he can handle.

The senior pastor keeps giving Charles more and more work because he knows that Charles will get it done. Charles is now doing several tasks outside of his regular responsibilities. Deacons refer hurting church members to Charles because they know he has genuine compassion for the hurting. Community members have learned Charles is the guy to see if you want a helping hand.

Suddenly, Charles no longer enjoys ministry. What makes matters worse is that Charles has been in ministry for only six months. Can he sustain this for another thirty years or more? What Charles needs is to get his priorities in order. He needs to determine what is most important in his life and ministry.

Priorities matter. Leaders can become overwhelmed when priorities are not set, as Charles did. Other church leaders have their priorities misaligned. This problem often takes the form of leaders thinking too highly of themselves. In recent years, there has been a string of stories of pastors who resigned or were forced out of their churches. In the past, this often resulted due to sexual sin or mishandling finances. However, the prevailing issue today seems to be centered around pastors putting themselves too high on the pedestal of power. It seems they have elevated themselves to such a position that their ministry teams and churches have taken a back seat to their own interests. This issue is just one way that a Christian leader can develop misplaced priorities. Leading the Jesus way means leading with proper priorities.

A Jesus-like leader must determine the most vital parts of their life and ministry. I try to take care of myself physically, but that's not nearly as important as maintaining personal time with the Lord. I try to be efficient with my time, but that should be secondary to stopping for a moment to give devoted attention to someone. We must prioritize integrity over style, character over charisma, and people over success. We must lead with the proper priorities. Leading with appropriate priorities is the Jesus way of leadership.

Leaders Must Prioritize Jesus

As we journey through these final pages of the book, we'll look at some Scriptures that I've already mentioned, and some I haven't. Many of these passages deserve another mention. It is evident from the New Testament that Jesus knew that he and his followers would face many challenges. Jesus said in Mark 13:9, "You will be handed over to the local councils and beaten in the synagogues. You will stand trial before governors and kings because you are my followers." Jesus continued in verse 9 and into verse 10, "But this will be your opportunity to tell them about me. For the Good News must first be preached to all nations." Jesus wanted his followers to tell others about *him*. Jesus-like leaders must prioritize Jesus. He wanted his followers to know that the task would not be a mere walk in the park, yet it *must* be carried out. Jesus fulfilled his mission despite opposition, and he called others to prioritize him even when they face opposition.

Another time, Jesus explicitly warned a large crowd about the challenges of following him. He challenged them to consider what it might cost them to follow him. Jesus said,

If you want to be my disciple, you must, by comparison, hate everyone else—your father and mother, wife and children, brothers and sisters—yes, even your own life. Otherwise, you cannot be my disciple. And if you do not carry your own cross and follow me, you cannot be my disciple.

But don't begin until you count the cost. For who would begin construction of a building without first calculating the cost to see if there is enough money to finish it? Otherwise, you might complete only the foundation before running out of money, and then everyone would laugh at you.

. . . So you cannot become my disciple without giving up everything you own. (Luke 14:26–29, 33)

Jesus knew that his ministry would lead to his death. He also knew that others would face hardship as they followed him. But he continued to lead and call others to forsake everything else to follow him. The costs of following Jesus may be great, but he is worthy of it all. Following him is worth it all.

Let's begin by understanding what we are getting into when we dive into Christian ministry. Christian ministry is not easy. We may lose opportunities, relationships, many hours of sleep, and even our lives. There will undoubtedly be challenges. But understanding the great value of following Jesus moves us to reprioritize our lives, even when facing challenges. The apostle Paul spoke of this reality in Romans 8:18 when he said, "Yet what we suffer now is nothing compared to the glory he will reveal to us later." Walking the ways of Jesus is not always easy, but it is the highest priority—and it is beautiful! Leaders who lead like Jesus will prioritize Jesus above all else.

Leaders Must Prioritize Heavenly Value

Jesus called his followers to treasure heavenly things over earthly things. He said, "Don't store up treasures here on earth, where moths eat them and rust destroys them, and where thieves break in and steal. Store your treasures in heaven, where moths and rust cannot destroy, and thieves do not break in and steal. Wherever your treasure is, there the desires of your heart will also be" (Matthew 6:19–21). It will be much easier to get our priorities in sync with the priorities of Jesus when we value what Jesus said to value. The treasures of this earth are sure to pass away, but the glories of heaven will remain forever.

We often learn what was essential to Jesus by the way he ministered. Consider the response of Jesus when four friends brought to him a paralyzed man on a mat. Mark tells us in Mark 2:5, "Seeing their faith, Jesus said to the paralyzed man, 'My child, your sins are forgiven.'" First of all, I imagine that if I were one of those who lugged that man around on a mat, I may wonder if the man would be any easier to carry since his sins were forgiven. After all, they probably expected Jesus to heal the man physically, not spiritually. However, Jesus knew what the man truly needed. Jesus prioritized the man's spiritual problem. The beautiful part of the story is that after the religious leaders questioned Jesus's authority to forgive sins, Jesus healed the man physically as well. Jesus demonstrated that he was not only powerful, but he was also authoritative.

Jesus also sought to reframe how "spiritual" people thought of faithfulness to God. Many religious people in Jesus's day were focused on outward appearances and religious behaviors. They concentrated on earthly signs of religion. Jesus pushed them to understand that what was inside mattered. "Healthy people don't need a doctor—sick people do," Jesus said, "Now go and learn the meaning of this Scripture: 'I want you to show mercy, not offer sacrifices.' For I have come to call not those who think they are righteous, but those who know they are sinners" (Matthew 9:12–13).

Consider also the parable of the rich man and the tax collector:

> Then Jesus told this story to some who had great confidence in their own righteousness and scorned everyone else: "Two men went to the Temple to pray. One was a Pharisee, and the other was a despised tax collector. The Pharisee stood by himself and prayed this prayer:

'I thank you, God, that I am not like other people—cheaters, sinners, adulterers. I'm certainly not like that tax collector! I fast twice a week, and I give you a tenth of my income.'

"But the tax collector stood at a distance and dared not even lift his eyes to heaven as he prayed. Instead, he beat his chest in sorrow, saying, 'O God, be merciful to me, for I am a sinner.' I tell you, this sinner, not the Pharisee, returned home justified before God. For those who exalt themselves will be humbled, and those who humble themselves will be exalted." (Luke 18:9–14)

The world may value things like prominence, pomp, and self-righteousness, but Jesus values humility, repentance, and dependence upon the mercy of God. As you seek to lead the Jesus way, do so in part by valuing the things of God over the things of this world.

Remind yourself of your salvation experience and your calling to ministry. Think back to when you were humbled even to be considered as a potential leader. Periodically journal about your calling to ministry and why you continue serving the Lord. Spend time praying and confessing sins while thanking God for the opportunity to serve his people. Let us be like Jesus. Let us value heavenly things over earthly things.

Leaders Must Prioritize Servanthood

Jesus-like leaders must make servanthood a top priority. Likewise, they must teach others to prioritize servanthood. God has called us to pursue something better than what this world has to offer and to lead *others* to do the same.

One way most people can refocus their priorities on servanthood is by thinking of themselves less. As Jesus led, he sought to teach his followers to redirect their focus from themselves to God and others (see Matthew 22:36–40). In Philippians 2 the apostle Paul spoke of this type of attitude that followers of Jesus should possess.

You must have the same attitude that Christ Jesus had. Though he was God, he did not think of equality with God as something to cling to. Instead, he gave up his divine privileges; he took the humble position of a slave and was born as a human being. When he appeared in human form, he humbled himself in obedience to God and died a criminal's death on a cross. (Philippians 2:5–8)

Many of the leaders in our world focus squarely on themselves. This focus is not the Jesus way. Jesus desires for us to lead as servant leaders. Jesus himself said, "Whoever wants to be first must take last place and be the servant of everyone else" (Mark 9:35). Last place: that's the place of the leader who leads like Jesus.

Ask yourself these challenging questions: Do you want to be first place, or do you put others first? Do you want others to serve you, or are you serving others? Are you developing your platform, or are you developing others? Do you desire the recognition of other people, or do you desire the approval of God?

Jesus not only commended servanthood to us, but he also modeled it. We have already seen Paul's writing in Philippians that Jesus humbled himself in obedience to the point of death on a cross. That's sacrifice. Jesus also gave his disciples a memorable display of servanthood in John 13:4–5. John writes, "So he got up from the table, took off his robe, wrapped a towel around his waist, and poured water into a basin. Then he began to wash the disciples' feet, drying them with the towel he had around him." Jesus went on to explain that this was not merely a beautiful display for them; this was an example of humility that he wanted them to follow. John continues a few verses later,

After washing their feet, he put on his robe again and sat down and asked, "Do you understand what I was doing? You call me 'Teacher' and 'Lord,' and you are right, because that's what I am. And since I, your Lord and Teacher, have washed your feet, you ought to wash each other's feet. I have given you an example to follow. Do as I have done to you. I tell you the truth, slaves are not greater than their master. Nor is the messenger more important than the one who sends the message. (John 13:12–16)

We may be tempted to think this act by Jesus was merely a great moral lesson for the followers of Jesus rather than something Jesus actually expects us to do. Don't fall into that temptation. There are very few displays of humility among the leaders of this world. Yet, this posture is what Jesus expects of his followers. This is the Jesus way of leadership.

Jesus actually raised the bar much higher than personal displays of humility. He spoke about extreme sacrifice in Mark 8:34–35. I wrote about this earlier in the book. In case you don't recall, "If any of you wants to be my follower, you must give up your own way, take up your cross, and follow me." How's that for a refocused priority? Leading the Jesus way means you must be willing to lay down your life to follow Jesus. So, as you lead like Jesus, don't try to promote yourself, increase your platform, and lead others toward your agenda. Instead, serve others, lead others to Jesus, and lead others to be like Jesus. That commitment may require you to refocus your priorities.

How, then, do we refocus our priorities on servanthood? Let us focus intensely on what is most important for followers of Jesus: Jesus himself. In the Gospels, a woman used an expensive jar of perfume to anoint Jesus. Some of the others in the room criticized her even though she was seeking to honor Jesus. Some thought the perfume could have been sold and used to feed the poor rather than "waste" its value. Listen to Jesus's response:

Leave her alone. Why criticize her for doing such a good thing to me? You will always have the poor among you, and you can help them whenever you want to. But you will not always have me. She has done what she could and has anointed my body for burial ahead of time. I tell you the truth, wherever the Good News is preached throughout the world, this woman's deed will be remembered and discussed. (Mark 14:6–9)

Jesus pointed out that he was the most significant focus for this woman. As we lead the Jesus way, Jesus should be the center of our focus. He must be our highest priority. So, as leaders who lead like Jesus, let us refocus our priorities on him, the perfect model of servanthood.

My relationship with God is the most important priority in my life. I owe everything to him. Second is my wife. She is my best friend and the love of my life. I'd do nearly anything for my wife. Third are my kids. I'd lay down my life for them in a heartbeat. They are my treasure and joy. After that comes my other family, my friends, and my church. I have a special relationship with these people—a relationship that goes above and beyond the world at large. Then I try to value other people, even strangers, above myself. This priority is what Jesus taught us to do in his Word.

Finally, I think about myself. I spend some time doing what I want to do. I rest, I read, I recreate. It's essential to think about myself, but it's not the most essential focus of my life; God and others come first as I seek to serve them. Likewise, God and others should come first in the lives of those who lead the Jesus way.

Leaders Must Prioritize the Big Picture

I've sometimes been frustrated while trying to lead our church. I want them to see that God wants to do something special in our church. Then I hear a complaint about the temperature of the sanctuary, the bulletin that had a small typo in it, or some other insignificant issue. When I face those moments, I sometimes want to scream, "Is your complaint really that important?" However, sometimes I also focus on the wrong issues. I may be giving too much attention to whether the signage looks perfect rather than focusing on if I have shown Christlike love to others. I may be more concerned with our church website than I am with whether our church family shares the gospel with our community. As those who lead the Jesus way, we need to intentionally focus on the big picture, namely, loving God and loving others.

Jesus was intentional as he ensured that his followers understood where their attention and energy should be focused. He helped his followers see the big-picture focus for following God's commands. We learned about this in chapter 3 when we talked about teaching simply. As a matter of review, Mark 12:28–34 says,

> One of the teachers of religious law was standing there listening to the debate. He realized that Jesus had answered well, so he asked, "Of all the commandments, which is the most important?" Jesus replied, "The most important commandment is this: 'Listen, O Israel! The Lord our God is the one and only Lord. And you must love the Lord your God with all your heart, all your soul, all your mind, and all your strength.' The second is equally important: 'Love your neighbor as yourself.' No other commandment is greater than these."

In addition to making this reality clear and straightforward, Jesus gave his followers something to focus their utmost effort and passion on: loving God and loving others. The big picture that Jesus wanted God's people to focus on was simple; it involved love, God, and people. This big-picture focus breaks through all the distractions that we face in our lives. If we focus on loving God and loving others, everything else will fall into its proper place.

At some point in my ministry I realized that I was making the teachings of God too complicated for others (and probably even for myself). When I realized that loving God and loving others was the most important of all of God's laws, it was like a breath of fresh air for my soul and my leadership. I discovered the most important priority for me and those I lead. I learned that leading like Jesus meant helping others see and live the big picture of God's ways.

Jesus was the master of focusing on the big picture. He had an uncanny ability to set aside the worries of this world and the distractions of minor matters to focus on the most important matters. For example, in Luke

10:38–42 he urged Martha not to worry about the household chores but to instead to focus upon what mattered (him). Or consider when he devoted specific time to prayer between the feeding of the five thousand and his miraculous walking on water (see Matthew 14:22–34).

Also, the disciples of Jesus may have felt ill-prepared to lead the church after Jesus left, but Jesus left them with great power (see Acts 1:8) and clear big-picture instructions. Shortly before he left the earth, Jesus gave his disciples the Great Commission. We looked at this in chapter 5, but let's consider it again. Jesus said in Matthew 28:18–20:

> I have been given all authority in heaven and on earth. Therefore, go and make disciples of all the nations, baptizing them in the name of the Father and the Son and the Holy Spirit. Teach these new disciples to obey all the commands I have given you. And be sure of this: I am with you always, even to the end of the age.

Again, Jesus was pointing to the big picture. What was most important for them to do was to continue his work of making disciples. This focus allowed the disciples to look past all the challenges they would face (and they would face many). They were then able to put their effort into doing the major task that Jesus left for them.

So, as you lead people, ask yourself, "Do I lead with the big picture in mind? Do I help my followers understand what is most important? Do I lead others to love God and love others?"

As a teenager I was recruited by a man at our church to sell warm pretzels and lemonade at a car racing event. After a long commute, we finally got to a vendor stand where we were to sell the pretzels and lemonade. The man in charge gave us what seemed like a thirty-second explanation of what to do: warm up pretzels, make lemonade, take money, and give out the food. That man left, and we never saw him again. Things started kind of slow, but they picked up quickly when there was a break in the action at the race. Suddenly, dozens of people were upon us, and we were slinging pretzels, squeezing lemons, and taking money. Honestly, I felt ill-prepared at first. However, we were successful. Our leader had instructed us to focus on what was most important for that task: pretzels, lemonade, and money.

Even as I write this book, in fact, our church is preparing to host an event for our community. When our church family asks why we are doing this, my reply is quite simple: "We want people to know that we love them." That's it. We're not trying to fundraise, nor are we trying to grow our attendance. We're not even trying to preach to those who come; we are simply trying to love people in an unmistakable way. That's the big-picture goal for this event. So, as you lead, learn to keep the big picture in the mind for yourself and those you lead. That is the Jesus way of leadership.

Leaders Must Prioritize Faithfulness to God

Jesus had many outstanding characteristics: he was humble, wise, compassionate, strong, holy, and much more (I could go on because, after all, he's divine). Still, one of the most beautiful traits of Jesus's leadership is his faithfulness. He was faithful to God the Father and the mission to which the Father had called him.

Jesus was so faithful to the Father and his mission that he told some he encountered he couldn't hang around too long because there was much work to be done. He said in Luke 4:43, "I must preach the Good News of the Kingdom of God in other towns, too, because that is why I was sent." He had a lot to do, bore a huge responsibility, and planned to be faithful to the task.

Yet, even amid all that Jesus had to do, he was faithful in spending time with God the Father. Luke records, "despite Jesus' instructions, the report of his power spread even faster, and vast crowds came to hear him preach and to be healed of their diseases. But Jesus often withdrew to the wilderness for prayer" (Luke 5:15–16). Mark says in Mark 1:35–37, "Before daybreak the next morning, Jesus got up and went out to an isolated place to pray. Later Simon and the others went out to find him. When they found him, they said, 'Everyone is looking for you.'" This moment teaches us that Jesus may have been busy and in high demand, but he was faithful in spending time with God in prayer and preparation.

And it was Jesus's time with the Father and his knowledge of the Word that prepared him to face temptation as a leader. During a time of fasting and prayer, Jesus faced great temptation from the devil (see Luke 4:1–13). We covered this biblical account when I wrote about the opposition that Jesus faced. Each time, Jesus responded with Scripture. Jesus said to the devil, "No! The Scriptures say, 'People do not live by bread alone.'" Again, "The Scriptures say, 'You must worship the Lord your God and serve only him.'" A third time, he said, "The Scriptures also say, 'You must not test the Lord your God.'" So, how are we to be faithful amid the devil's deception? We are to return to the truths and promises of God's Word, as Jesus did. Leading the Jesus way means being faithful to God and his ways, particularly in the face of temptation.

Even as Jesus approached the most monumental moment of his earthly life, he did not neglect time with the Father; he prioritized it. I'm sure it's an understatement to say that Jesus was uneasy about the events leading up to his crucifixion. Being uncertain about something can keep you awake at night. I don't know about you, but I'm usually an excellent sleeper. My wife will often have to wake me to check on one of our boys if there is some problem. However, I do occasionally have trouble sleeping. This sleeplessness often comes whenever I'm facing an event or decision that is exciting or unnerving. Can you imagine how Jesus must have felt the evening before he was crucified? The Scriptures give us a picture of what Jesus was experiencing during this time.

> Then Jesus went with them to the olive grove called Gethsemane, and he said, "Sit here while I go over there to pray." He took Peter and Zebedee's two sons, James and John, and he became anguished and distressed. He told them, "My soul is crushed with grief to the point of death. Stay here and keep watch with me."

He went on a little farther and bowed with his face to the ground, praying, "My Father! If it is possible, let this cup of suffering be taken away from me. Yet I want your will to be done, not mine."

Then he returned to the disciples and found them asleep. He said to Peter, "Couldn't you watch with me even one hour? Keep watch and pray, so that you will not give in to temptation. For the spirit is willing, but the body is weak!"

Then Jesus left them a second time and prayed, "My Father! If this cup cannot be taken away unless I drink it, your will be done." When he returned to them again, he found them sleeping, for they couldn't keep their eyes open.

So he went to pray a third time, saying the same things again. Then he came to the disciples and said, "Go ahead and sleep. Have your rest. But look—the time has come. The Son of Man is betrayed into the hands of sinners. (Matthew 26:36-45)

In this intense time with the Father, Jesus specifically prayed, "I want your will to be done." Jesus wanted the Father's will to be done, not his own, even though he recognized the horrific experience that awaited him. In fact, the contrasting actions of his disciples highlight Jesus's faithfulness in this moment. What were they doing? Sleeping soundly. Surely they were all tired, perhaps even scared and confused. But no one had more on their shoulders than Jesus did. Still, he was faithful.

No doubt, the most fantastic display of Jesus's faithfulness was his death on the cross. In Philippians 2:7–8, the apostle Paul said that Jesus "gave up his divine privileges; he took the humble position of a slave and was born as a human being. When he appeared in human form, he humbled himself in obedience to God and died a criminal's death on a cross." Obedience to God. Faithfulness to God. Leading the Jesus way means that commitment to God takes priority over your personal priorities and the world's priorities.

Leading like Jesus means prioritizing being faithful to the Father, even when others are not. So, ask yourself these questions to help you remain faithful to God and his ways: "Do my decisions reflect that God is most important in my life? Does the Bible indicate that my decision is faithful to God and his ways? What is my will in this situation, and how does it compare to God's will? How can I be more like Jesus when he prayed, 'Yet I want your will to be done, not mine?'"

What are your priorities as a leader? Stop for a moment and ponder that question. The priorities valued by many leaders today are money, power, influence, platform, legacy, and the like. What Jesus valued was much different. First and foremost, Jesus prioritized his relationship with and obedience to God the Father. He didn't live for this world; he lived for the kingdom of God. Why are you on this earth? Why do you want to lead? With which priorities will you lead?

If you and I will lead the Jesus way, we will need to recalibrate and refocus our priorities. Our calling of ministry and our walk with Jesus are too valuable for us to focus on less important matters. So, learn to prioritize what is most important. Keep your mind on the things of God. Put your energy into reaching the high calling of loving God and loving others. Lead with proper priorities. Lead the Jesus way.

Leaders Must Prioritize with the End in Mind

As a pastor, I have sat in many meetings . . . many meetings. Sometimes our meetings get so bogged down in particulars and the urgency of the moment that we forget what we are working toward. We get so hung up on what type of blinds go in our building that we forget that we're trying to introduce people to the Light of the world. We get so caught up in talking about something on social media that we forget that our church should offer true intimacy and connection with others. Sometimes we forget where we should be going.

Jesus led with the end in mind. Leading with the end in mind means that we keep the ultimate goal of the situation in the forefront of our minds as we lead. Jesus knew how to do this; he knew the vital reason he came to the earth, and it shaped his life and ministry. Consider his focus in Luke

9:51: "As the time drew near for him to ascend to heaven, Jesus resolutely set out for Jerusalem." Resoluteness—that's what we need to lead with the end in mind.

Of course, Jesus knew the end of the story perfectly. Jesus frequently told his disciples how events would unfold. He knew he would be rejected, crucified, and raised to new life (see Luke 9:21–22). Knowing why he came to the earth helped keep Jesus focused on his day-to-day ministry, which in turn helped him keep his disciples focused.

Leading with the end in mind was crucial to Jesus as he led with proper priorities. You may be tempted to think, "Yeah, but I'm not Jesus. I don't know exactly why I'm here or what I'm supposed to do. How can I lead with the end in mind?" Well, the thing is, we *do* know why we are here. Jesus gave us the Great Commandment and the Great Commission. We *do* know the end of the story. The Bible tells us that Jesus will return and God will make all things right (see Revelation 21:4). Also, Jesus has told us that he is with us always (see Matthew 28:20). God won't leave us to ourselves. Nothing can separate us from his love (see Romans 8:38–39). So, lead with confidence. Lead with the end in mind. Lead the Jesus way.

I've had to remind myself of this principle many times in my own leadership. I began pastoring the church where I currently serve a little over five years ago. Now, let me be clear: I love our church. I love our people. I love pastoring this flock that God has given me to lead. By God's grace, right now, our church is healthy and thriving. However, our church was suffering five years ago. There were many heartbreaking issues and many problems that plagued our church. I faced some of the most challenging encounters of my entire ministry in my first few days on the job. I knew, though, that God had called me to our church, and I knew that God could bring new life and new love to our church in a miraculous way. I knew that God had a great end in mind for our church. Leading with the end in mind sustained my wife and me in those early days at our church.

Leading with the end in mind means that a new pastor doesn't lose his cool with one angry church member, because that pastor knows God can use his faithfulness (in part) to do something beautiful with a local church. Leading with the end in mind will help a fresh missionary stay the course when language studies become frustrating, because she knows that God means to reach people from every language, tribe, and nation with the hope of forgiveness in Jesus (see Revelation 7:9). Leading with the end in mind means that a faithful couple leading a youth small group will continue to pray for the new students in their group, because they know God can work powerfully through loving relationships and his Word will not return void (see Isaiah 55:11). Leading with the end in mind is leading the Jesus way.

Conclusion

Charles, our youth pastor friend from the beginning of the chapter, has started to learn how to get his priorities in order. Jesus is most important in his life, and he wants to keep it that way. However, he's come to understand that faithfully serving Jesus doesn't mean you must burn out along the way. Charles has determined his priorities begin with his personal relationship with God. Outside of his relationship with Jesus, Charles's most important relationship is with his new wife.

After God and his wife, Charles has committed himself to serving in ministry with excellence. While serving at his church, Charles identifies which aspects of his job are most important by meeting with his senior pastor to set goals and determine strategies. He wants to be humble and willing to serve in any area, but he doesn't want to spread himself too thin. Charles wants to love the Lord, love his wife, and love his church for a long time. So, Charles has started to set himself up for years of healthy ministry. He's started to lead the Jesus way. You can, too.

Key Takeaways from This Chapter:

1. Leading the Jesus way means prioritizing Jesus.
2. Leading the Jesus way means valuing heavenly things more than earthly things.
3. Leading the Jesus way means prioritizing servanthood.

4. Leading the Jesus way means focusing on the big picture.
5. Leading the Jesus way means being faithful to God.
6. Leading the Jesus way means leading with the end in mind.

Action Steps for Leaders

1. Spend time in God's Word and describe what Jesus called his followers to do.
2. Make a list of what you value most. How does it compare to what the Bible calls us to value?
3. Think about your biggest priorities for this week. Should those priorities be most important to you?
4. Identify the big-picture items in your life. Are you spending your time and attention on those items?
5. Ask some seasoned pastors what kind of end they desire for their life and ministry. What can you learn from them?
6. Create an action plan to be faithful in your life and ministry. Review that plan once a month.

It's Time to Lead the Jesus Way

"The right leader can cause someone to charge hell with a water pistol." I've heard that expression several times over the years. I'm not sure where that statement originated, but it's catchy. Although it is theologically sloppy, it is a good illustration of the power of influence a leader can have over someone.

Jesus was that kind of leader and much more. Jesus said to Peter, "Upon this rock I will build my church, and all the powers of hell will not conquer it" (Matthew 16:18). Jesus inspired and equipped Peter and the other apostles to lead the church and begin a movement that would carry on for thousands of years. Indeed, the forces of hell would feel the impact of the leadership of Jesus in the lives of his followers. That's effective leadership.

You can't be like Jesus in every way, but you can in many ways, including in how you lead. You can lead as one who prioritizes people in a way that is beautifully contradictory to this world. You can sacrificially meet needs as you lead. You can be an effective and wise teaching leader. You can be a leadership developer and multiplier who perpetuates a leadership legacy. You can boldly lead in the face of opposition. You can lead with God-centered and God-shaped priorities.

Jesus has not only modeled for us how to lead in these ways, but he has also sent his Holy Spirit to empower us to lead in these ways. Jesus said in John 14:16, "And I will ask the Father, and he will give you another Advocate, who will never leave you." God's Spirit is your advocate, and he will never leave you. So, lead with confidence and lead in Christlikeness.

Surely there will be some challenges as you lead like Jesus. The Jesus way involves facing and overcoming those challenges. Anticipate challenges, and continue to lead. When you're tired, weak, or fearful, remember that you're not leading by your own strength. When you face resistance, remind yourself that you are in good company: Jesus and the other great leaders of history met opposition.

If leadership were easy, many more would lead. Consider what type of leader you want to be, especially when you are tempted to make your leadership about yourself. Do you want to build a kingdom of your own, or do you want to be a part of what God is doing in his kingdom? Don't let the challenges you face slow you down; use them as a reminder that you're on the right path. Keep leading.

Perhaps you're ready to begin leading the Jesus way, but you don't know where to start. Maybe you've never led before, or perhaps you've been leading the wrong way for quite a while. Start small. Set some goals for how you can lead the Jesus way now. Review the key takeaways from each chapter. Choose one key task from each of the six chapters and focus on those steps for the next six weeks. For example, for week one, you may choose to pray that God would make you someone who prioritizes people. For week two, you might ask someone to gently point out to you if you are being impatient. For week three, you could identify some ways you could improve your teaching in your various leadership contexts. For week four, you can establish clear expectations for those you have equipped to lead. For week five, you might consider how to respond to opposition in a godly way. And for week six, you could identify some big-picture items in your life.

Once you've begun taking these first steps, add to your Christlike leadership repertoire as you go. God is still shaping you into the leader he called you to be. Keep leading.

A Final Challenge

I've wanted to be a leader for as long as I can remember. Something about showing others a better way and helping others develop has always drawn me. However, for many years I was spinning my wheels without going anywhere. I was even going in the wrong direction at times. I witnessed domineering leaders in politics. I learned from arrogant leaders in athletics. I was even exposed to misguided leaders in local churches.

Thank God, though, that through his Word and the influence of many Christlike leaders, I came to discover the Jesus way of leadership. Now, by God's grace, I seek to lead people to walk in the way of Jesus, and I strive to be a leader who walks in the way of Jesus. It's only by God's continual patience with and development of me that I am glad to share what I've learned with others. We're all a work in progress; we're all a part of God's marvelous work in his people.

The task for Christian leaders is grand. Jesus said in the Great Commission that we are to go, make disciples, baptize them, and teach them to follow and obey him (see Matthew 28:18–20). Jesus also said that we will be his witnesses all over the world (see Acts 1:8). The mission that Jesus gave us is monumental and challenging. However, Jesus has not left us to ourselves. Instead, he has equipped us with everything we need to achieve the task, and he has modeled for us how we are to lead through the task.

This mission needs leaders who are prepared to be used by God to do great things for his kingdom. Are you ready to lead? If so, lead on, leader.

Lead the Jesus way.

Guideposts for Leading the Jesus Way

1. Leaders like Jesus prioritize people.
2. Leaders like Jesus see and meet needs.
3. Leaders like Jesus teach people.
4. Leaders like Jesus develop people.
5. Leaders like Jesus lead despite opposition.
6. Leaders like Jesus prioritize what's important.

Notes

1 Andy Stanley (@AndyStanley), "People Are Hesitant to Abandon the Status Quo," Twitter, February 17, 2021, https://twitter.com/andystanley/status/1362026270658281474.

2 Andrew Hébert, "Shaping Church Culture: Table Fellowship and Teaching in Luke-Acts," (EdD diss. The Southern Baptist Theological Seminary, 2015), 78.